Growing Pains: The Making of America's Middle School Teachers

Growing Pains

The Making of America's Middle School Teachers

by
Peter C. Scales and C. Kenneth McEwin

Commissioned by
The DeWitt Wallace-Reader's Digest Fund

NATIONAL MIDDLE SCHOOL ASSOCIATION
AND
CENTER FOR EARLY ADOLESCENCE

nmsa ®

NATIONAL MIDDLE SCHOOL ASSOCIATION

The DeWitt Wallace-Reader's Digest Fund provided a generous grant which made possible the research studies presented and analyzed in this monograph. The Center for Early Adolescence (University of North Carolina at Chapel Hill) and the National Middle School Association are grateful to the DeWitt Wallace-Reader's Digest Fund for this support and are pleased to publish jointly this important report.

Finally, of course, both associations are appreciative of the scholarship and competence of Drs. Peter Scales and Kenneth McEwin, the authors of the report. Dr. Scales is the Director of National Initiatives for the Center for Early Adolescence, School of Medicine, University of North Carolina at Chapel Hill. Dr. McEwin is Professor of Curriculum and Instruction, Appalachian State University, Boone, North Carolina and a Senior Consultant to the Center for Early Adolescence.

ISBN 1-56090-083-0

Table of Contents

List of Figures

List of Tables

Acknowledgments

Many people have helped us conduct this study and prepare this report. We thank especially the DeWitt Wallace-Reader's Digest Fund whose generous support has made this research and the Center for Early Adolescence teacher preparation initiative possible. We are most grateful for the support of Donna Dunlop, former Program Manager for the DeWitt Wallace-Reader's Digest Fund, who saw the need for an initiative to strengthen middle level teacher preparation and helped us conceptualize the role of our research in that larger initiative, and for the continuing support of Mildred Hudson, who became the Fund's Project Officer for this project.

The assistance of Tom Dickinson was invaluable. Now at Indiana State University, he was editor of the *Middle School Journal* for the National Middle School Association, and spearheaded the collaboration between NMSA and the Center for Early Adolescence. He also reviewed an early draft of the manuscript. April Tibbles, Managing Editor of the *Journal,* ensured that the sample recruitment letters and questionnaires were printed accurately and professionally. John Lounsbury, Director of Publications for NMSA, served as final editor and with the help of Mary Mitchell, was responsible for designing and producing this publication. We are grateful too for the support of Sue Swaim, Executive Director of NMSA, who gave her encouragement of this collaboration.

At the Center, Director Frank Loda was an energetic supporter of this research and gave it a high priority in the Center's overall program.

Operations Manager Suzanne Rucker supervised the mailing and receiving of thousands of questionnaires, with the assistance of Secretary Terry Hammersley. Rucker and Hammersley spent many hours helping with the revision of the instrument as well as managing the mailing and receipt of the completed questionnaires. Both also helped to prepare this report. Computer Systems Manager Bobbie Sanders worked with Master Key, Inc. of Chapel Hill to ensure the accurate entry of data for subsequent analysis. Sanders also helped conduct the statistical analyses and create the report's graphs. Jim Rosinia, Director of Information Services, and Roberta Lloyd, Information Specialist, made sure that we had access to all relevant literature.

We would also like to thank Doris Jenkins, Associate Dean of the College of Education and Sara Zimmerman, Chair of the Department of Curriculum and Instruction, Appalachian State University, for their encouragement and support. Without their cooperation this project would not have been possible.

Finally, we want to thank the thousands of middle school principals and teachers who participated in this study. They are often asked to complete questionnaires such as ours, and the large number who did so, despite the time participation took, ensured that we had a strong research base from which to draw our conclusions. Their willingness to participate and to comment—more than 1,000 teachers, half of our sample, provided comments on different questions—was the heart of our research. We hope we have shared their perspectives accurately. They will have a significant impact on the way the coming generations of middle level teachers are prepared. To them, we owe our deepest gratitude.

—Peter C. Scales
—C. Kenneth McEwin

May, 1994

Foreword

It is gratifying indeed to read and comment upon this significant study by Scales and McEwin. Their prior work is such that another collation of data with its report and interpretation carefully presented is to be expected, and is certainly presented here. Readers well-grounded in educational statistics will find their painstaking reporting of the data satisfying, while those not so inclined can readily identify the important conclusions.

To those of us long associated with middle school development, it is somewhat disappointing to learn how slowly the percentage of middle school teachers with specific middle level preparation has grown. Yet it is satisfying to note that the programs are becoming more comprehensive. It is encouraging too, to learn that the large majority of middle grades teachers plan to stay in the middle level classroom for the remainder of their careers for positive reasons such as enjoyment of teaching this age group and the desire to "make a difference" in their lives. Only seven percent of teachers indicated they wanted to leave the middle grades classroom for reasons that could be considered negative. We have no greater need than successful experience in teaching at the middle level.

Disappointing, however, is the finding that while more than half of the teachers in the study had some kind of special preparation for teaching young adolescents, the majority received it in their graduate programs, with only about one in five having an undergraduate program in middle school education. Our teacher education institutions have been much too slow to develop and promote middle level teacher education in undergraduate programs. Those of us who are promoters of middle school teacher education must work harder to convince university authorities and certification agencies of the importance of offering a middle school specialization to teacher education entrants. This study will provide a valuable new tool for us to carry out that mission.

Of course, much of the overall problem lies in the fact that the number of middle schools has almost mushroomed in the last two decades, after most of the faculties of teacher education institutions already had their own teacher education for elementary or secondary education. So, we must encourage teacher education colleges to employ middle school teachers to share their experiences with today's middle level students. With graduate programs in middle level education steadily improving, the supply of teachers for their programs should also steadily increase.

The authors' recommendations as to the 10 points middle grades education programs should serve seem appropriate. They are sound and, if implemented, would ensure that teachers of young adolescents would be well-prepared for the broad, awesome responsibilities they face in today's middle schools.

—William M. Alexander

I.

The Status of Middle Level Teacher Preparation

In 1992, the Center for Early Adolescence released *Windows of Opportunity: Improving Middle Grades Preparation* (Scales, 1992a). That report described an eight-state study which included data from 439 randomly selected fifth through ninth grade teachers, 86 deans and directors of middle grades teacher preparation programs, and the chief state school officers of seven of the eight states.

Some major findings from that study were: (a) Only 17% of the teachers had received special middle level preservice preparation for teaching at the middle level; (b) almost one-half rated as inadequate or poor their preparation on 11 specific topics considered important for middle grades teachers; and (c) those teachers who had special middle grades preparation were only somewhat less likely to give such low ratings to their teacher preparation. That study was the most extensive of its kind to date at that time. It was the largest sample of middle grades teachers asked to evaluate their preservice preparation, and the first sample in the literature that was randomly selected. Because it filled these gaps, the Windows Study, data, and recommendations for strengthening middle grades teacher preparation have been widely disseminated and discussed (Scales, in press; 1993; 1992a; 1992b).

In the three years since those data were collected, several additional studies have been published or are in preparation, that provide additional information regarding middle level teacher preparation and certification. "4000 Voices" provides information from 4000 middle level teachers who responded to a questionnaire included in an issue of the *Middle School Journal* (Page, Page, & Dickinson, 1992). *The Professional Preparation of Middle Level Teachers* (McEwin & Dickinson, in press) profiles middle level teacher preparation programs from 14 institutions across the nation and provides additional information for those planning new middle level teacher preparation programs or evaluating and improving existing ones . Additionally, Swaim and Stefanich are working on a national project sponsored by the National Middle School Association that focuses on selected exemplary program components which correspond to those found in the National Middle School Association/National Council for Accreditation of Teacher Education-Approved Curriculum Guidelines for middle level programs.

Valentine, Clark, Irvin, Keefe, and Melton (1993) conducted a study of middle level principals for the National Association of Secondary School Principals which reported data on principals' perceptions of teachers' professional preparation. Specifically, they found that only 11% of teachers in their sampled schools held a middle level certificate. Moreover, only 36% of principals in 1992 estimated that their teachers had university coursework that "focused on middle level education," versus 44% found in a similar NASSP study in 1981. Valentine and Associates reported an even bigger apparent drop in student teaching at the middle level, with only 32% of the principals saying their teachers had this type of preparation in 1992, versus 58% of principals who felt that way in

1981. These researchers offered no explanation for this puzzling finding, but two possibilities might be bias introduced by selective response rates, and the fact that these were principals' perceptions, not the reports of teachers themselves about their own preparation.

A very comprehensive study of 1,798 middle level schools (McEwin, Dickinson, & Jenkins, in press) conducted during the 1992-93 school year found a similar lack of progress in the specialized preparation of middle level teachers. Sixty-one percent of the respondents from middle schools, predominantly principals, estimated that less than 25% of faculty members at their schools had specialized middle level teacher preparation. Furthermore, only 9% of the respondents believed that over 75% of teachers at their schools had such preparation. A similar 1987-88 national study (Alexander & McEwin, 1989) found identical percentages of 61% and 9% indicating a complete lack of progress, at least as measured by the perceptions of principals.

This apparent lack of progress in the impact of middle level teacher preparation occurred over a decade in which the rhetoric about strengthening that preparation increased. During that same time period, a national survey of teacher preparation institutions belonging to the American Association of Colleges of Teacher Education found that 33% offered specific middle level teacher preparation programs as compared to 38% in 1991. The 1991 study also found that only 33% of all teacher preparation programs, including those that were not members of AACTE, had special programs for the preparation of middle level teachers. However, the apparent quality of these programs increased during this time same period (Alexander & McEwin, 1988; McEwin & Dickinson, in press). Overall, other data do not indicate a dramatic decline in either the likelihood of teachers being prepared in special programs or in the quality of those programs, but rather minor fluctuations in both quantity and quality of middle level teacher preparation.

Despite these and other reports, the *Windows of Opportunity* study (Scales, 1992a) remained the largest and most rigorous study of middle grades teachers' views on their own preparation. However, some teacher educators raised concern about the study related to one of the key findings. Since few significant differences in preparation program ratings were reported between those who had received specialized middle level preparation and those who had not, there was some concern that opponents of special middle level teacher preparation programs could use these findings to block the development and implementation of specialized programs. There was also some concern regarding the large number of fifth grade teachers that responded to the study and the relatively low response rate.

In the search for university resources, existing programs usually have the upper hand over new proposed programs, and schools/departments of education generally have less internal leverage for obtaining campus support than other schools or departments (Goodlad, 1990). Thus, within the politics of the university, there must be solid evidence to bolster the case for new or expanded education programs, especially if a new program would take resources from existing elementary and secondary programs. In this context, the mixed findings of the Windows Study on how favorably those with specialized preparation rated their middle level programs were a disappointment to persons ideologically committed to such programs.

Unfortunately, in the Windows Study, the data were not sufficient to determine which respondents had received specialized preparation in comprehensive programs and those who had received preparation in weak, less comprehensive ones. For example, some respondents may have attended programs that had only one or two middle level courses and few, if any, field experiences with young adolescents. Other respondents, however, may have completed full, four-year programs comparable to those who major in elementary education. Thus, the special middle level preparation program designation covered a range of quality, and the more numerous weak programs could have obscured the potential positive impact of the less common strong programs. That is, graduates of strong, comprehensive middle level programs might have rated their preparation more favorably, but such ratings would have been undetectable in that study.

Yerian and Grossman (1993) provide some support for this possibility in their study of graduates of the University of Washington Puget Sound Professional Development Center program for middle level preparation. They compared 30 special middle level program graduates with 44 elementary/secondary program graduates who were placed in middle schools for their student teaching. Special program graduates had some specific components that defined their program: a team-taught block of courses on middle school teaching and learning, a semester-long field experience at a middle school, and supervision by a middle school teacher. All these components were among those the earlier sample felt characterized strong middle level preparation programs. The special middle level program graduates felt significantly more prepared than the other graduates to work with middle level students and felt more knowledgeable about young adolescents and their needs. The findings must be viewed with caution since the sample sizes were so small and because the special program graduates were volunteers who may have entered the program already different from the comparison group on their senses of preparedness and their readiness to ascribe favorable ratings to special study of the middle level. Nevertheless, the data lend credence to the possibility that the effects of comprehensive programs were understated in the earlier study.

The Current Study

To respond to the concerns teacher educators raised about the earlier study, and to help fill these gaps in the research literature, the Center for Early Adolescence, with the cooperation of the National Middle School Association, designed another study intended to increase the response rate over the previous research and to gather more data to distinguish the self-reported impact of high quality programs from lesser quality programs.

This monograph details that study and highlights its implications for strengthening middle level teacher preparation. In addition, the results of several other Center for Early Adolescence activities undertaken since the Windows Study are presented. These include: a Delphi Study of experts to prioritize the Windows recommendations; a study of Middle Grades Teacher Educators; and, trends from the Center's work with three university/middle school collaboratives. These data are used to describe the impact that middle level teacher preparation programs seem to have and what they need to do to strive for excellence in preparing the next generation of middle school teachers.

The quality of middle level teacher preparation does seem to be improving, but the progress is both slow and uneven. Like the development of young adolescents, the making of America's middle school teachers is a process filled with fits and starts, and not a few "growing pains." Educators, youth workers, and policymakers now understand how to promote positive young adolescent development. Through the perspective of the 2,139 teachers included in this study, more is now known about ways to promote the positive development of the nation's middle level teachers. It is time now, as the poet William Wadsworth Longfellow wrote, to "let us then be up and doing."

II.

Planning for the 1993 Study: What Experts Recommend Should Be Done To Strengthen Middle Level Teacher Preparation

The *Windows of Opportunity* study (Scales, 1992a) reported fifth through ninth grade teachers' views on how middle grades teacher preparation can be strengthened. Another source of information about necessary actions is a modified Delphi process the Center for Early Adolescence conducted in 1992. In spring 1992, 77 university-based teacher educators, state education officials, middle grades teachers and administrators, and representatives of national education organizations and foundations were asked to rate the 33 recommendations from the *Windows of Opportunity* study. The respondent pool was comprised of members of the Center's 56 person teacher preparation project advisory panel (made up of leading middle grades teacher educators, researchers, policymakers, and foundation representatives), several additional teacher educators with considerable reputations in the middle grades community, and middle school practitioners in several urban areas who were serving as leaders in another Center middle grades school restructuring project. The pool was balanced by race and gender, and included individuals from all regions of the country.

This pool was invited to participate in a two-step Delphi Study. In the first step, respondents received a questionnaire that listed the 33 recommendations. They were asked to rate on a 5-point scale each recommendation on two dimensions: (1) the degree to which the individual personally agreed with the recommendation, and (2) how important the individual believed the recommendation to be in strengthening middle grades teacher preparation. Respondents were also able to provide extended comments if they wished. Responses were received from 59 individuals (77% response rate).

Center staff members tallied the responses to determine which recommendations were both agreed to and considered to be the most important. To be selected for the next round of the Delphi, an item had to receive *1's* and *2's* (the two most favorable ratings) from at least 70% of the respondents. Twelve items met this criterion. In the next step, the 59 individuals who responded to the first questionnaire were mailed a second one. This time, they were asked to rank order the 12 items, giving *1* to the item they thought was the most important, *2* to the item they thought was the second most important, and so on. Additionally, they were asked to give their reasons for assigning the ranks they did. Responses were received from 42 individuals. Thus, the total response rate for the two stages of the Delphi was 55%. Eighteen responses were received from university-based teacher educators, 10 from representatives of national organizations and foundations, and 7 each from state departments of education and from middle grades teachers, administrators, and preservice teachers.

The rankings of the 12 most important items are displayed in Table 1 with the mean score also included. One point was given for a ***1,*** two points for a ***2,*** and so on. Thus, an item that received ten ***1***s, nine ***2***s, eight ***3***s, seven ***4***s, and six ***5***s would have a score of 110/40=2.75. It should be remembered that these were the items rated most important

TABLE 1

Expert Delphi Ranking of Recommendations for Strengthening Middle Grades Teacher Preparation

Rank	Score	Recommendation
1	3.76	Greater understanding of early adolescent development with special attention to young adolescents' social relationships and self-awareness, greater emphasis on responding to cultural and language diversity, more coverage of teacher-based guidance, and more coverage of how to involve parents/family members and community resources in young adolescents' schooling
2	4.45	Greater variety of developmentally responsive teaching and assessment techniques, especially cooperative learning, interdisciplinary curriculum and team teaching, student exhibitions and portfolios
3	4.90	Middle grades teacher education should expose 1st and 2nd year preservice middle grades teachers to extensive experiences in effective and successful middle grades schools with a diversity of young adolescents
4	5.43	Middle grades teacher preparation programs should incorporate more opportunities for preservice teachers to learn how to utilize family and community resources and to observe (through case study, personal communication, and visits) communities which systematically meet the varied needs of young adolescents
5	5.81	Middle grades teacher education programs should make more extensive use of cooperating school teachers in developing teacher preparation coursework and in the continuing education of middle-grades teacher educators
6	6.17	Mechanisms should be established for middle grades teachers, principals, other school district staff, and middle grades teacher educators to rapidly access information about early adolescence and model school and teacher education programs, and to network nationally with one another

TABLE 1 (CONT)

Rank	Score	Recommendation
7	6.20	Middle grades teacher preparation programs should include significantly more opportunities for pre-service teachers to sharpen their skills in advocating for the "whole young adolescent" and for multidisciplinary programs/services
8	6.60	Middle grades teacher preparation programs should have earlier, lengthier, and more varied field experiences
9	6.71	Research should be conducted to determine what criteria reliably and validly distinguish high quality from lesses quality (minimum standards) middle grades teacher preparation programs
10	7.24	A working group of educators should be established to ensure the explicit recognition of middle grades issues in broader education reform initiatives and to stimulate the leadership needed to carry those issues forward
11	8.36	Support and assistance should be provided to the National Association of State Directors of Teacher Education and Certification initiative to strengthen their middle grades standards
12	9.02	Awareness of state middle grades professional associations and NMSA should be raised among middle grades professionals

1=very important; 5= not at all important

out of an initial 33. Although some items ranked lower than others in the final ranking, all were considered important by the respondents.

Items 6 and 7, and 8 and 9, are close enough in mean score to be considered ties, but the other items are sufficiently differentiated from each other to consider their relative rankings to be reliable and valid.

We used the results of the *Windows of Opportunity* study and this Delphi to inform the 1993 study of middle school teachers and their preservice preparation reported in this volume.

III.
The 1993 Study of Middle Level Teacher Preparation

In the Center's earlier study, middle level teachers from eight states were randomly selected to provide a range of teacher preparation environments. States chosen included those with historical commitments to middle grades teacher preparation and advanced college/university programs as well as those whose commitment was just emerging (see Scales, 1992a for details). In the present study, we were more interested in examining the impact of high quality programs and therefore focused only on states where there would be a high likelihood that participating teachers had graduated from more comprehensive programs.

We wanted to sample only from those states that had "authentic" middle level teaching certificates, i.e., certificates that were separate and distinct from elementary or secondary ones (Valentine & Mogar, 1992) and that had a relatively large number of middle level teacher preparation programs that were major specializations, not just endorsements or add-ons to elementary or secondary programs.

In addition, we wanted to select states where there was some overlap in certificates covering the middle grades so that responses from teachers with "authentic" certificates could be compared with those who had middle grades included in their elementary or secondary certificate. These considerations led us to select the following states for the sampling frame:

1. Georgia
2. Kentucky
3. Missouri
4. North Carolina
5. Virginia

Among them, at the time of sampling, these five states contained 57% of all undergraduate middle level teacher preparation programs in the country (McEwin & Dickinson, in press).

Market Data Retrieval, Inc., a company that maintains extensive national educational mailing lists, was used to identify the principals of all grades 6-7-8 configured middle schools in all five states. This configuration was selected because the largest number of teachers with special middle level teacher preparation teach in grades 6-8 schools (McEwin & Dickinson, in press) and because the majority of all young adolescents in the United States attend grades 6-8 middle schools (Epstein & Mac Iver, 1990).

To increase the response rate over the 1991 survey (data collected in 1991, publication occurred in 1992), the 1993 questionnaire was shortened considerably and included very few questions with open-ended responses. The 1993 survey instrument was also professionally printed and mailed in attractive NMSA envelopes. Six surveys were enclosed with individual return envelopes in a packet addressed to each school's principal. Principals were asked to select six teachers to complete the surveys from among those teaching language arts, science, mathematics, and social studies in grades 6, 7, and 8, and to select teachers so that a variety of grade levels and subjects would be represented. The subject areas mentioned above were chosen because middle level teachers teaching other subjects rarely have had special middle level preparation.

Pre-addressed post cards were enclosed for principals to complete and send to the Center for Early Adolescence. They were asked to indicate how many teachers received the survey and the grade levels and subjects taught by those teachers. This was our means of knowing how many teachers actually had a chance to complete a survey, and thus was important for computing the response rate. Principals were instructed that, if teachers taught more than one subject area, they were to be counted in the subject they taught most frequently. If they taught equally in two or more areas, principals were to randomly assign them to one subject area and not count them twice. The same guidelines applied if a teacher taught more than one grade level.

A total of 1,100 grades 6-8 schools were identified in the five states and packets were mailed to the principals in late March, 1993. A follow-up letter was sent in early May to schools that had not responded.

Results

By the cutoff date of early July 1993, the Center for Early Adolescence had received postcards from 525 principals, a 48% response rate distributed as displayed in Table 2 (percentages do not add to 100 because of rounding):

As in the Center's earlier teacher preparation study, North Carolina had the highest response rate, possibly because of the Center's location in that state. Except for North Carolina's higher rate, the states had response rates ranging from 41% to 49%. If each state had equal numbers of responding schools, each would account for 20% of the total response.

As Table 2 shows, however, Kentucky and Missouri responses are under-represented, because the number of middle schools in those states was smaller. However, compared to the proportion that their number of middle schools represented in the original population, the responding sample percentages were very close. North Carolina had a slightly higher proportion in the sample than in the original population, and Kentucky and Georgia had slightly lower respondent proportions, with Virginia and Missouri's respondent sample identical to their proportion in the original population. Thus, although the response rates varied among the states, the distribution by state of the responding sample proved to be within a few percentage points of the distribution of the original population.

TABLE 2
Middle School Response Rate Among the States

State	Identified	Responding	Rate	Original%	Total%
Georgia	270	120	44	25	23
Kentucky	148	60	41	13	11
Missouri	174	85	49	16	16
North Carolina	287	153	53	26	29
Virginia	221	107	48	20	20

Within these schools, principals distributed questionnaires to a total of 2,705 teachers [941 sixth grade (35%), 918 seventh grade (34%), and 846 eighth grade (31%)]. The sample included 846 language arts teachers (31%), 622 science teachers (23%), 573 social studies teachers (21%), and 644 mathematics teachers (25%). A total of 2,139 middle school teachers returned questionnaires for a response rate of 79%. The prevalence of teaming and curriculum integration in middle schools meant that the majority of our sample taught more than one subject and often more than one grade level. It was impossible to legitimately assign them to one grade and/or one subject for analysis purposes. Therefore, we did not analyze the data by those variables. Unless otherwise indicated, the following results are based on the final sample of 2,139 responding middle school teachers.

Demographics

The sample was overwhelmingly female (82%) and white (90%). (Figures 1 and 2) These findings, however, are not dramatically different from national statistics which show that 88% of all teachers in grades K-8 are female and that 87 percent of all public school teachers are white (National Center for Educational Statistics, 1993a; 1993b).

Figure 1

Gender of Respondents

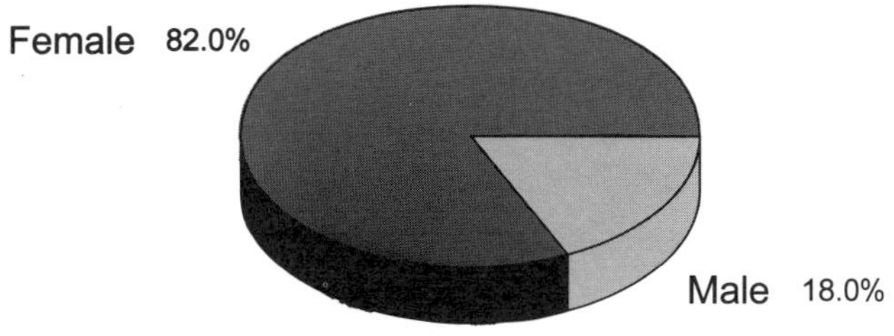

Figure 2

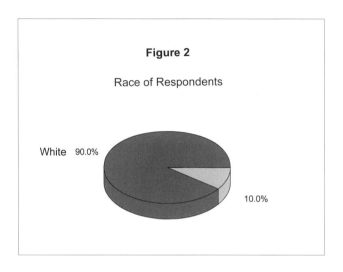

Race of Respondents

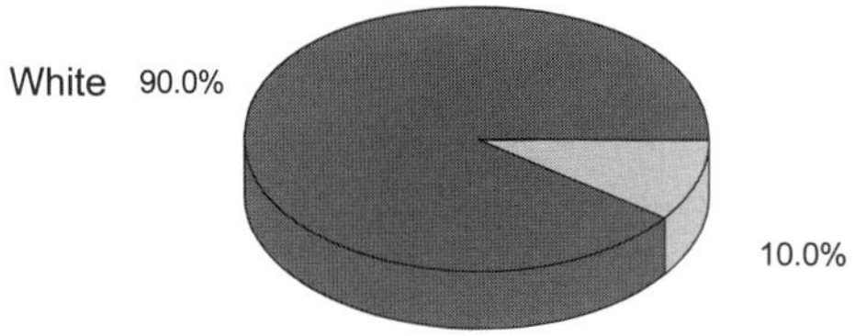

Nearly one-half of the sample (47%) taught in rural areas, 31% in suburban areas, and 22% in urban settings. This compares with national statistics which indicate 50% (40,000) of public schools are in rural and small towns, 26% in urban fringe and large towns (21,000), and 24% (19,000) in central cities (NCES, 1993b, p. 5). (Figure 3)

More than six in ten of these middle school teachers (63%) did not initially intend to teach in the middle grades. Fifty-three percent had been teaching in the middle grades for nine years or less, and more than a fifth (22%) had been teaching young adolescents for three years or less. (Figure 4) In comparison, the average years of experience of all teachers in the country is 15 (NCSS, 1993b, p. v). Of the 51% who had at some time taught at the elementary or secondary levels, half had taught at the elementary level, and 18 % at the secondary level.

Figure 3

Community Type

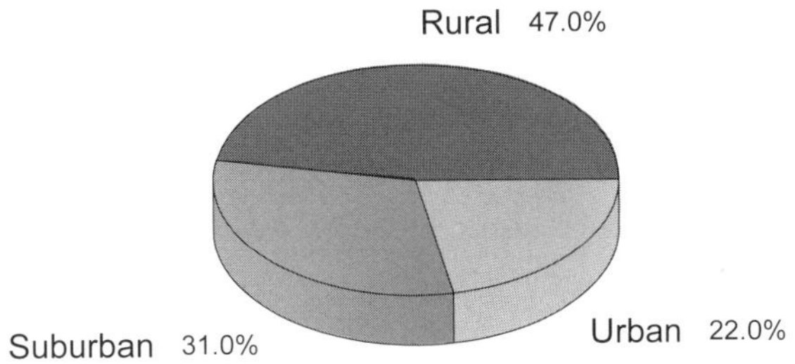

Figure 4

Years Teaching in Middle Grades

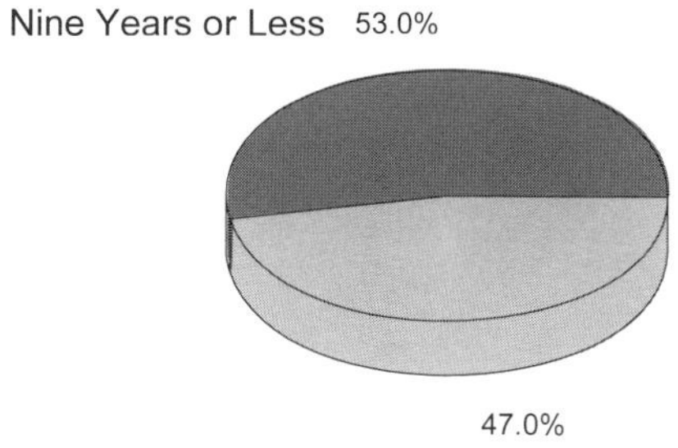

Respondents could list up to three teaching certificates they held. Nearly half of the sample (49%) listed as their first certificate an "authentic" middle level certificate, one that did not include large overlaps into elementary or secondary grades (e.g., 4-8, 6-9). Among the remainder, 16% held a "middle/secondary" certificate (e.g., 6-12), and 12% held an "elementary/middle" certificate (e.g., K-8). Of the 57% of the sample who had more than one certificate, 17% listed an "elementary/secondary" (e.g., K-12), 15% listed an elementary/middle level certificate, 12% had an elementary/secondary certificate, and 10% held an authentic middle level certificate. Sixty-five percent of those listing three certificates (47%) held an authentic middle level one.

Respondents were also asked to indicate the subjects in which they were certified, but this item produced a large non-response: only 41% of the sample said they were certified in a particular subject. Among this group, 31% were certified in social studies, 19% in English/language arts, 18% in science, and the remainder in other subjects. The fact that at least one of the five states does not certify teachers in specific subject areas possibly contributed to the low response rate on this item.

Principals were asked to distribute the questionnaires only to teachers of English/language arts, mathematics, sciences, and social studies. A greater percentage of teachers stated they taught these subjects than said they were certified in them. According to their responses on this item, 41% indicated they "regularly" taught English/language arts, 34% taught mathematics, 32% sciences, 35% social studies, 30% reading, and 11% other subjects. Respondents could indicate all of the subjects they taught, and so responses could add to more than 100%. There was almost no non-response to this item, and so these responses to subjects "regularly" taught appear to provide more accurate data about teachers' content areas than do the responses to the question about certificates held. It could also be that many teachers are teaching content areas in which they do not hold certificates.

Fifty-nine percent of the sample were members of the National Middle School Association, 9% as individuals and 50% because their schools were institutional members (17% of the sample did not respond to this question).

Special Middle Level Preparation

To increase the accuracy of our data compared with the 1991 study, we asked for information about respondents' initial, most recent, and undergraduate preparation. Just 23% said they received their initial teacher preparation in a middle level program. Similarly, as expected, just 22% said they had received their undergraduate preparation "in a program specifically designed for middle grades teaching." (Figure 5) However, a sizeable majority of the 56% who had a graduate degree said their most recent preparation was for the middle level (67%). (Figure 6) Among those who did not receive their preparation in a special middle grades program, the great majority (71%) believed there was no special program available at the time.

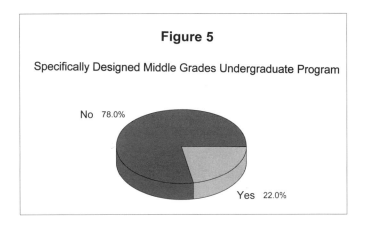

Figure 5

Specifically Designed Middle Grades Undergraduate Program

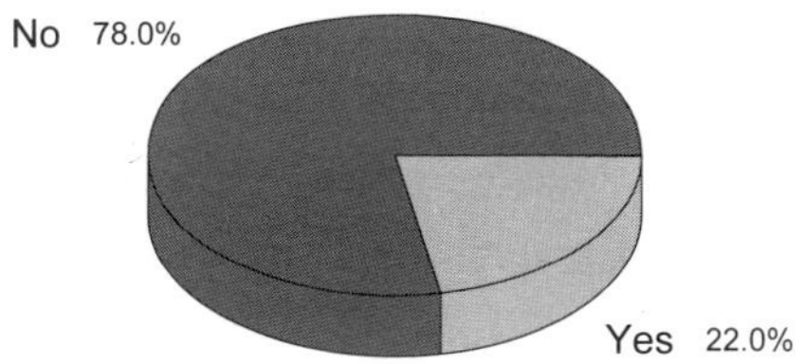

Figure 6

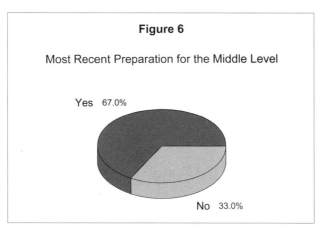

Most Recent Preparation for the Middle Level

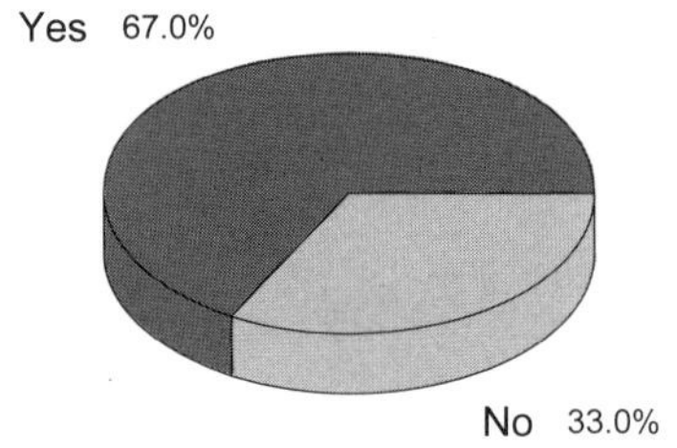

The chances that a teacher's initial preparation was in a special middle grades program appear to have increased over time. The sample was divided into those who received their bachelor's degree in 1978 or earlier, and those who had received them between 1979-1985, 1986-1990, and 1991 or later. Those with more recent degrees were moderately more likely to have been in a special middle grades program (Chi-square 218.33, with 3 degrees of freedom, significant at the .000 level, lambda of 1.5%, and Spearman correlation of —.34).

Respondents were asked to indicate the number of courses and the number of semester hours (estimated if necessary) they took in their initial middle level certification program that "focused directly on teaching in the middle grades (5-9)." Student teaching hours were not to be counted in these totals. Both of these items had high non-response rates and so the results might be misleading: 18% of the sample failed to report how many courses they had taken, and 38% did not indicate how many hours they had taken. Among those responding, 65% (53% of the total sample) took 4 or fewer "specialized" middle level courses: More than a third of those responding (36%; 29% of the total sample) had no specialized middle level courses. At the other end of the spectrum, 15% of those responding (13% of the total sample) stated that they had 11 or more specialized courses.

Among those who indicated they took many courses, some of these courses were probably not full quarter or semester length, for the semester hours respondents said they took did not parallel the number of courses they said they took—just 3% of the respondents took more than 18 hours of course work, the equivalent of 6 semester-long courses, and yet 19% said they had taken more than 6 courses! At the lower end, hours more nearly paralleled courses. Half of the respondents (51%) took 12 or fewer hours, close to the 53% who said they took four or fewer courses. Nearly 3 in 10 (29%) had no semester hours of specialized middle level courses, the same percentage as said they had no courses.

Comprehensiveness of Preparation

In addition to asking about the number of courses and the semester hours in respondents' middle level programs, several other questions were asked to help determine the comprehensiveness of the programs from which these middle school teachers graduated. Questions about the coursework and field experiences, including student teaching, were included. The teachers' responses (Table 3) suggested that most of these middle school teachers graduated from programs that did not have much depth of the middle level content.

Ratings of Preparation Programs

Respondents were asked to rate the adequacy of their professional education programs in preparing them on six content items repeated from the *Windows of Opportunity* study and one new item, with the results shown in Table 4.

TABLE 3

Courses Focusing On Selected Middle Grades Topics and Experiences

Courses and Experiences	Percents	
	Yes	No
Course work focusing on:		
* Young adolescent development	69	31
* Curriculum and organization of the middle school	46	54
* Appropriate methods for teaching young adolescents	58	42
* Teaching reading at the middle level	50	50
* Concentration in at least two academic areas at the undergraduate level	58	42
* Were academic concentrations broad and interdisciplinary	62	38
* Pre-student teaching field experiences in the middle grades	42	58
* Student teaching in the middle grades	44	56

*These components were used to determine comprehensiveness.

TABLE 4

Percent of Teachers Citing Less Than Adequate Preparation

Topics	Percent
Understanding young adolescent development	26
Using effective instructional techniques at the middle level	35
Middle level curriculum and organization	43
Using effective cooperative learning/ techniques/grouping practices	47
Responding to student's cultural and language diversity	57
Teaching on an interdisciplinary team	61
Being an advisor in a teacher-based guidance program	73

Sample

The 1993 sample had a slightly higher percentage of female teachers and rural teachers than the 1991 sample, and a somewhat smaller proportion of teachers who worked in suburban and urban areas. The 1993 sample was also somewhat less experienced: in the 1991 sample, more than half had taught in the middle grades for more than 10 years, while in the 1993 sample, less than half had. Finally, a higher percentage of the 1993 sample were members of NMSA. In 1991, teachers were not asked about institutional membership, and the great majority of 1993 respondents were members through this plan.

The 1993 sample of middle-grades teachers was purposely selected from grades 6-8 configured middle schools in the five states with the majority of the country's middle-grades preparation programs, whereas the 1991 sample included teachers who taught grades 5-9 in any middle grades configuration, selected from states that included both extensive and limited middle grades preparation programs.

Thus, our sampling frame was designed to maximize the likelihood that respondents would have had special preparation for teaching in the middle grades, and made it more likely that they would be NMSA members as well. A greater percentage of the 1993 sample did report having had special preparation. Even so, just 22% of the 1993 sample said they had received their undergraduate preparation in a special middle-grades program, compared with 17% who had special preparation in the 1991 survey.

However, in the 1991 survey, the most recent professional preparation was not investigated. In the 1993 survey, we obtained a more complete picture and found that those middle grades teachers who went on to obtain masters or higher degrees were much more likely to enroll in a special middle grades preparation program. Adding undergraduate and graduate preparation together, it can be estimated that 55% of these middle school teachers had some kind of special preparation at one of these levels: 22% received it at the undergraduate level and an additional 33% whose undergraduate preparation was not in a middle level program did receive special preparation at the graduate level. This figure may be overstated, however, because we asked about undergraduate programs that were "specifically designed" for the middle level, while the question on the most recent preparation asked, less precisely and strongly, whether the teachers had been in a "middle level program." It is also not known what percentage of the sample taught for a year or more before obtaining graduate level preparation.

This is a welcome finding, for it suggests that a sizeable proportion of teachers whose undergraduate background is not in the middle grades, but who end up teaching in those grades or who wish to do so, are enrolling in special middle grades preparation programs at the graduate level.

Ratings of Program Quality

Nevertheless, nearly half of this large representative sample of middle school teachers have not had special preparation at either the undergraduate or graduate level, and the quality of the total 1993 sample's preparation programs was not rated more highly than the 1991 sample's programs. Nearly a third of the respondents' professional preparation programs, including both undergraduate and graduate levels, did not even include coursework on young adolescent development, more than 40% did not include coursework focusing directly on appropriate methods for teaching young adolescents, more than half did not cover the curriculum and organization of the middle level school, and nearly 60% did not include any fieldwork or student teaching experiences in grades 5-9.

Given these data, it is not surprising that a mean of 50% of the teachers rated as inadequate or poor their preparation on seven specific topics considered important in middle grades teacher preparation programs. As in the 1991 survey, majorities rated as inadequate or poor their preparation in:

- cooperative learning
- responding to students' cultural and language diversity
- interdisciplinary teaming
- teacher-based guidance programs.

Even considering young adolescent development, 26% felt this core content was inadequate or poorly covered, nearly the same percentage (28%) as felt that way in the 1991 survey (Figure 7).

Figure 7

PERCENT RATING PREPARATION LESS THAN ADEQUATE
1991 AND 1993 SAMPLES

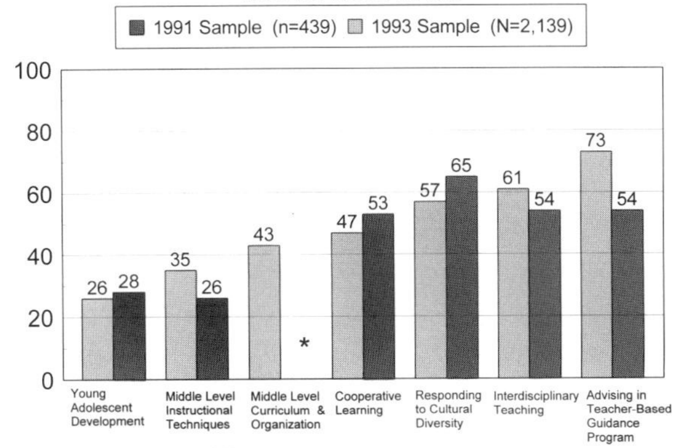

* No direct comparison in 1991

Thus, the proportion of teachers with special preparation at the undergraduate level, though low in absolute terms, was substantially higher (22% versus 17%) when comparing the 1993 and 1991 samples. The 1993 sample, however, was expressly selected to make that outcome more likely. If anything, the 1993 results probably overstate the percentage of teachers in states other than these five who have received special undergraduate preparation. Moreover, there is no evidence that these middle school teachers, more of whom had special preparation than the 1991 teachers, and all of whom were teaching in a grades 6-8 middle school, rated their preparation for teaching the middle grades any better than the 1991 sample. Despite the sampling differences between the 1991 and 1993 samples, and despite the 1991 sample's relatively low response rate of 28% (versus the more substantial 1993 rate of 48%), Figure 7 shows that while there are some differences by topic in how inadequate the total 1991 and 1993 samples of middle grades teachers rated their preparation for teaching in the middle grades, the overall depiction of less than adequate preparation is virtually the same for both samples.

Did Specially-Prepared Teachers Have More Comprehensive Preparation Programs?

The total 1993 teacher sample differed little from the total 1991 teacher sample on how they evaluated their preparation for teaching young adolescents. As in 1991, we were interested in whether those teachers who had special middle grades preparation would evaluate their preparation more favorably than those who did not have special preparation.

First, however, we wanted to determine whether the preparation for those with special middle grades preparation programs was any more comprehensive than for those who did not have this special preparation. We identified seven coursework and field experiences that the literature commonly suggests middle grades teachers should have in their background, such as special coursework on young adolescent development and student teaching specifically in middle level schools. Respondents were asked whether they had experienced seven different components in their preparation program, and responses of those with such special preparation were compared with the responses of those with elementary or secondary preparation. The seven comprehensiveness components were looked at both separately, and grouped into categories of high, medium, and low comprehensiveness. A program was defined as being highly comprehensive if it contained six or all seven of the course and field-work components, as medium if it contained three to five components, and as low in comprehensiveness if it contained two or fewer components. Figure 8 clearly shows that those teachers who were prepared in special middle grades programs were more likely to have comprehensive programs than teachers prepared in elementary and secondary programs.

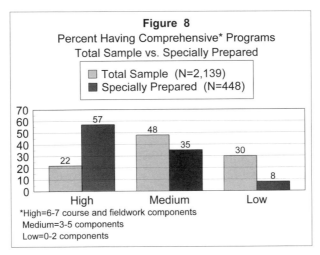

Figure 8
Percent Having Comprehensive* Programs
Total Sample vs. Specially Prepared

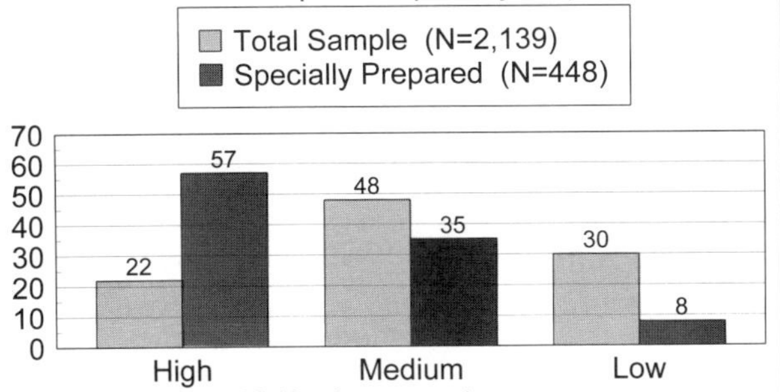

*High=6-7 course and fieldwork components
Medium=3-5 components
Low=0-2 components

Examining the data further, it was discovered that those prepared in special middle-grades programs were more likely to have had each of these seven program components as shown in Figure 9.

Next, several 2 X 2 cross-tabulations were computed to determine if these differences were statistically significant. Again, middle grades

Figure 9
Comprehensiveness of Preparation
Percent Having Selected Components

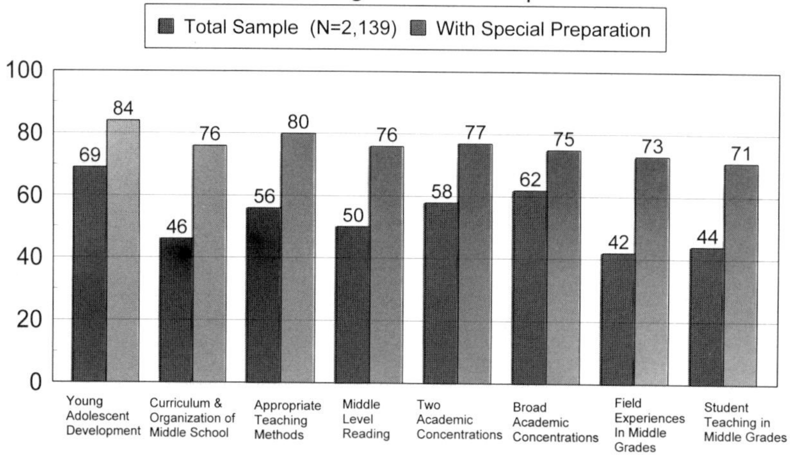

programs were more comprehensive. In fact, those teachers whose initial professional preparation (96% of "initial" preparation was in an undergraduate program) was in a special middle grades program were significantly more likely to have had each of the seven preparation program components, especially:

- coursework focusing specifically on the curriculum and organization of middle schools
- coursework focusing on teaching reading to young adolescents
- field experience in middle level schools
- student teaching in middle level schools.

TABLE 5

Preparation with Having Specific Program Components

Component	Chi-square	DF	Sig.	Lambda%	Spearman
Coursework on early adolescent development	64.84	1	.000	0	-.18
Coursework on curriculum and organization of middle schools	216.49	1	.000	26	-.33
Coursework on appropriate teaching methods	122.80	1	.000	0	-.25
Coursework on teaching reading	169.70	1	.000	25	-.30
Two academic concentrations	88.52	1	.000	0	-.21
Field experiences in middle grades	249.00	1	.000	26	-.36
Student teaching in middle grades	168.41	1	.000	22	-.29

DF=degrees of freedom; Sig.=significance level; Lambda=reduction in error predicting one variable when know value of the other; Spearman=correlation between ranks of ordinal variables (in this table, a negative correlation indicates that those with special middle-grades preparation were more likely to have had this component in their preservice program).

All these data (Table 5) indicate consistently that teachers who were prepared in special middle grades programs were significantly more likely than other teachers to have had each of these preparation programs components. For four of the components, the associations were moderately strong. Lambdas ranging from 22% to 26% mean that, if one knew that a respondent had received special middle grades preparation, one could reduce by 22% to 26% the error from chance guessing in predicting whether the respondent had coursework focusing on the curriculum and organization of middle schools and the other three components with these lambdas. Even those with 0 lambdas, suggesting a complete absence of predictive error reduction, at least had weak Spearman rank correlations with having had special preparation. Thus, we conclude there is indeed a moderate relationship between the initial preparation having been special middle grades preparation and the comprehensiveness with which the preparation program addressed key middle grades concerns.

Not surprisingly, those whose initial preparation was in a special middle grades program were also more likely to hold an "authentic" middle level certificate that had only minimal overlapping with elementary and/or secondary grades (Chi-square=245.67, with 2 degrees of freedom, significant at .000, lambda of 0%, Spearman correlation of .31).

To obtain a different perspective, relative risk estimates were also computed. The relative risk estimate provides a measure of how much more likely a respondent was to have had each of the program components depending on whether his or her initial preparation was in a special middle grades program or not. Across all seven components, those in middle grades programs were from 1.2 to 1.5 times more likely, or 20% to 50% more likely, to have had such comprehensive exposure.

The data were also analyzed depending on whether respondents' most recent or graduate preparation was in special middle grades programs or not. Similar significant findings were found, albeit weaker in each case, for four of the components, but teachers whose most recent preparation was in a special middle grades program were no more likely than others to have had a concentration in at least two academic areas, or either field experiences or student teaching in middle grades schools. These findings were expected, however, since most masters degrees are limited to one year's work and do not usually include sufficient hours to permit two or more academic concentrations. Similarly, middle level field experiences, including student teaching, are not usually required since the large majority of masters degree candidates are either part-time students who already teach in the middle grades or have done so before becoming a graduate student.

The number of preparation courses and the number of semester hours respondents had devoted to the middle level were examined to determine whether they would be associated with having comprehensive programs. As might be expected, the more courses devoted to the middle level that respondents had in their initial preparation program, the more likely the program was to have been highly comprehensive, as displayed in Table 6.

TABLE 6
Association of Number of Middle Level Courses with Program Comprehensiveness*

Comprehensiveness	Chi-Square	DF	Sig.	Lambda%	Pearson
With total comprehensiveness	607.06	14	.000	.17	.54

* Comprehensiveness categories: high=6-7 of the program course and fieldwork components; medium=3-5 components; low=0-2 components; Lambda=reduction in error predicting one variable when know value of the other; Pearson=correlation coefficient when both variables are interval scale.

This is a strong finding, indicating that the more courses preservice teachers take devoted to the middle level, the more likely they are to report their program was highly comprehensive. Moreover, the greater the number of courses devoted to the middle level, the more favorably respondents rated their middle level preparation programs on each of the topics investigated (Table 7).

TABLE 7
Association of Number of Middle Level Courses with Ratings of Program Adequacy

Topic	Chi-Square	DF	Sig.	Lambda %	Pearson
Young adolescent development	394.21	35	.000	.54	-.36
Effective middle level instructional techniques	450.93	35	.000	0	-.38
Middle level curriculum and organization	563.43	35	.000	7	-.42
Teaching on an inter-disciplinary team	314.23	35	.000	14	-.32
Being an advisor in a teacher-based guidance program	191.21	35	.000	8	-.24
Responding to students' cultural and language diversity	167.98	35	.000	5	-.23
Effective cooperative learning/grouping practices	245.14	35	.000	3	-.28

* In this analysis, a negative Pearson correlation indicates that those with more courses devoted to the middle level rated their programs more favorably. DF=degrees of freedom; Sig.=significance level; Lambda=reduction in error predicting one variable when know value of the other; Pearson=correlation coefficient when both variables are interval scale.

Did Specially-Prepared Teachers Rate Their Preparation Programs More Favorably?

One measure of program quality is the comprehensiveness of the program, as demonstrated by the participation of preservice teachers in various kinds of coursework and field experiences. As reported above, from that perspective teachers whose initial preparation was in a special middle grades program had higher quality (i.e., more comprehensive) programs. Another measure of quality is respondents' subjective, retrospective evaluation of how adequately their program prepared them to teach young adolescents.

It was reported above that a mean of 50% of the total sample rated as inadequate or poor their preparation on seven topics considered important for middle-grades teachers to know, including six items from Scales 1992 study. What difference did having had special middle grades preparation make on these ratings of adequacy?

The total sample was divided into those whose initial preparation was at the middle level and those who had any other kind of preservice preparation, and cross-tabulations were computed, with the results shown in Table 8. For all seven topics, significant chi-squares were found, but with low or zero lambdas, suggesting that, although those who had special middle-grades preparation were somewhat more likely to rate their programs favorably than were other teachers, the strength of these associations were quite weak (the large sample size could have produced statistically significant chi-squares of limited practical significance).

The eta coefficients also indicate that the relationship between ratings of program quality and having had special middle grades preparation are weak. Squaring eta provides a measure of the proportion of total variability in the dependent variable (the topics) that can be accounted for by the independent variable (in this case, having had special prepara-

Table 8
Association of Having Special Middle-Grades Preparation with Ratings of Program Adequacy

Topic	Chi-Square	DF	Sig.	Lambda %	Eta
Young adolescent development	120.16	5	.000	0	.20
Effective middle level instructional techniques	140.49	5	.000	0	.21
Middle level curriculum and organization	193.16	5	.000	0	.24
Teaching on an interdisciplinary team	97.62	5	.000	5	.16
Being an advisor in a guidance program	72.05	5	.000	4	.12
Responding to students cultural and language diversity	62.29	5	.000	0	.12
Effective cooperative learning/grouping practices	64.82	5	.000	0	.13

DF=degrees of freedom; Sig.=significance level; Lambda-reduction in error predicting one variable when know value of the other; Eta-correlation for use when dependent variable is interval scale and independent variable is nominal or ordinal

tion or not). The strongest association is .24, which when squared indicates that just 6% of the ratings' variability on middle grades curriculum and organization can be accounted for by knowing whether someone was initially prepared in a middle grades program or not.

A similar analysis was conducted using the most recent preparation as the independent variable, and similar results were obtained, but with even weaker lambda and eta coefficients. The only exceptions were the ratings on how well programs covered diversity and being a teacher-based guidance advisor, and these ratings were not significantly different between those who had been in a middle grades program and those who had not.

Impact of Program Comprehensiveness on Ratings of Adequacy

One of the key questions that could not be answered in the 1992 Scales study was what difference the quality of a middle grades preparation program made in teachers' ratings of program quality. We knew that middle grades program graduates as a group were not very different on most ratings from their peers who had other kinds of preparation. However, we suspected that relatively few teachers had been prepared in a high quality (comprehensive) program, and that the positive ratings they might have given those programs were statistically obscured by the more numerous poor programs to which teachers gave lower ratings.

The present study had two different measures of program depth, the number of different coursework and field experience components respondents had "focusing directly" on the middle grades, and the number of courses and semester hours they had that "focused directly on teaching in the middle grades (5-9)." These measures were used to determine if levels of program comprehensiveness were related to different ratings on program adequacy.

The sample was divided into three groups: those who had zero to 2 of the seven program coursework and field components (30% of the total sample), those who had 3 to 5 components (48% of the sample), and those who had 6 or all 7 components (22% of the sample). A one way analysis of variance for each of the seven topics on which ratings of adequacy were sought was then conducted to determine if the number of components respondents had in their programs was associated with differences in their mean ratings of adequacy for the various program topics.

For each of the seven topics, significant F-ratios were obtained, indicating that the three groups' mean ratings did differ. The Scheffe multiple comparison test was applied to determine the source of the difference. The Scheffe test is more conservative than other multiple comparison tests and requires that differences be larger than other tests require in order to be found statistically significant. For all seven topics, we found that those with 6 or all 7 program and field experiences ("high" comprehensiveness) had significantly more favorable program ratings than those with 3 to 5 program components ("medium"), and that those with 3 to 5 program components in turn gave significantly more favorable program ratings than did those with just 2 or fewer program components ("low") (Table 9). Thus, teachers who had more comprehensive programs rated those programs more favorably. An analysis of variance was then conducted only on the 23% of the sample whose initial preparation was in special middle grades programs to see if program comprehensiveness was still associated with significantly more favorable program ratings with the results shown in Table 10.

As for the total sample, teachers who had been prepared in highly comprehensive, special middle grades programs gave significantly more favorable ratings to their programs, on each topic, than teachers who had been prepared in special middle grades programs that had either medium or low comprehensiveness. Unlike the total sample, however, the medium group and low group did not differ in their ratings on cultural diversity, interdisciplinary teaming, and advisor-advisee programs. For these three topics, even specially prepared middle grades teachers rated their preparation inadequate if their program overall was of medium or low comprehensiveness.

TABLE 9
Mean Adequacy Ratings By Program Comprehensiveness
Total Sample

Topic	High*	Medium**	Low
Young adolescent development	1.53	2.00	2.75
Effective middle level instructional techniques	1.74	2.22	2.96
Middle level curriculum and organization	1.73	2.35	3.22
Effective cooperative learning/ grouping practices	2.13	2.60	3.17
Responding to students' cultural and language diversity	2.42	2.88	3.18
Teaching on an interdisciplinary team	2.30	2.90	3.55
Being an advisor in a teacher-based guidance program	2.83	3.32	3.77

* High group significantly different from medium and low groups at .05 level on all topics.

** Medium group significantly different from low group at .05 level on all topics.

Relationship Between Authentic Middle Level Certificates, Program Comprehensiveness, and Perceived Preparation Program Adequacy.

It has already been noted that those whose initial preparation was in a special middle grades program were moderately more likely to hold an "authentic" middle level certificate, one with minimal overlapping into elementary and secondary grades. The sample was divided into those

TABLE 10

Mean Adequacy Ratings By Program Comprehensiveness, Middle-Grades Graduates

Topic	High*	Medium	Low
Young adolescent development	1.47	2.01**	2.47
Effective middle level instructional techniques	1.69	2.11**	2.65
Middle level curriculum and organization	1.69	2.15**	2.64
Effective cooperative learning/grouping practices	2.08	2.68**	3.29
Responding to students' cultural and language diversity	2.38	2.86	3.03
Teaching on an interdisciplinary team	2.23	2.90	3.29
Being an advisor in a teacher-based guidance program	2.84	3.27	3.59

* High group significantly different from medium and low groups at .05 level on all topics.

** Medium group significantly different from low group at .05 level on these topics only.

who indicated that their first certification was authentically for the middle level (e.g., 4-8, 7-9, 6-8), those who had elementary/middle and middle/secondary certificates (a "divided" group, e.g. K-8, 7-12) and those with any other certificate (a "non-focused" group, e.g. K-12, K-5, 9-12). Since the authentic category was focused on the middle level, the divided group should have had less focus than the authentic but more than the non-focused group, and the non-focused group might have included the middle grades but with such a large span that special focus was less likely. An analysis of variance was performed on each of the course and fieldwork components of comprehensiveness. We had hypothesized that those who held authentic certificates would have a more comprehensive program, and this hypothesis was supported. Significant F-ratios were obtained for all comparisons and the Scheffe procedure revealed that the authentic group was more likely to have had each of the program comprehensiveness components as shown in Table 11.

We were somewhat surprised that the divided group was not significantly more likely than the non-focused group to have had any of these program comprehensiveness components. We had reasoned that a K-8 or 7-12 emphasis, versus a K-12 or purely elementary or secondary focus, would have made it more likely for middle grades content and techniques to have been covered, but this was not the case. Moreover, the non-focused group was significantly more likely than the divided group to have "coursework focusing on teaching reading at the middle level." This was probably due to two factors. The non-focused group contained a higher proportion of elementary teachers, who would be more likely than secondary teachers to have special reading courses and it also contained all those specifically certified in reading, thereby inflating this response.

We also wanted to know what the association was of having an authentic middle level certificate with respondents' ratings of their program adequacy. The same three groups were used—authentic middle level, divided, and non-focused certificates—and a one way analysis of variance with each of the program topics was run. In all but the case of

TABLE 11
Mean Program Comprehensiveness by Authenticity of Certificate

Topic	Authentic*	Divided	Non-Focused
Coursework on early adolescent development	.78	.60	.64
Coursework on curriculum and organization of middle schools	1.20	.66	.65
Coursework on appropriate teaching methods	2.07	1.43	1.51
Coursework on teaching reading at the middle level	2.56	1.39	1.85**
Two academic concentrations	3.27	2.55	2.48
Field experiences in the middle grades	2.94	2.04	2.47
Student teaching in the middle grades	3.52	2.86	2.76

Maximum score on topics was "1" for early adolescent development and "7" for student teaching.

* Authentic group significantly more likely at .05 level to have had each component than either of the other two groups.

** Non-focused group more likely at .05 level to have had this component than divided group.

diversity, the authentic group rated their programs significantly more favorably than either the divided or non-focused group. As before, the divided and non-focused groups were, except for diversity, not different from each other in the ratings they gave to their preparation programs (Table 12).

TABLE 12
Mean Adequacy Ratings by Authenticity of Certificate

Topic	Authentic	Divided	Non-Focused
Young adolescent development	1.93*	2.39	2.28
Effective middle level instructional techniques	2.15*	2.60	2.53
Middle level curriculum and organization	2.21*	2.82	2.68
Effective cooperative learning/grouping practices	2.58*	2.83	2.81
Responding to students' cultural and language diversity	2.76*	3.10	2.95**
Teaching on an interdisciplinary team	2.80*	3.22	3.18
Being an advisor in a teacher-based guidance program	3.24*	3.58	3.47

Ratings: 1=topic covered very well, 5= not at all.

* Authentic Group significantly more favorable at the .05 level than either of other two groups on these topics.

** Non-focused group significantly more favorable at the .05 level on this topic than divided Group.

It was disappointing that the divided group was not significantly different from the non-focused group on any of these topics. In fact, the non-focused group rated their programs' coverage of diversity issues more favorably than the divided group. No ready explanation for why this might be true is apparent. It may be that elementary prepared teachers are receiving more coverage regarding diversity issues than are secondary teachers. Since elementary certified teachers were overrepresented in the non-focused category, that could explain the result, but this is purely conjecture.

The principal result from this analysis is clear: those who had authentic middle level certificates were more likely to have had special middle level preparation and to have been in comprehensive programs, and, if their programs were highly comprehensive, were more likely to give favorable ratings to their programs' coverage of the seven topics considered crucial for effective middle level teaching. Later, we consider the implications of these results for how middle level teacher preparation programs should be structured and what experiences they should include. First, however, we report teachers' comments on various issues raised in the survey.

IV.

Teacher Voices: Comments and Open-Ended Responses

Respondents were asked to indicate whether or not they intended to continue teaching at the middle level for the remainder of their careers. They were also asked to indicate why or why not. A total of 1,069 teachers followed the "yes" or "no" response with reasons for their decisions. These responses were placed into the categories of *positive, neutral,* and *negative* with the following results: Positive responses 746 (70%); neutral responses 265 (25%); and negative responses 58 (5%). Sample statements from the positive, neutral, and negative responses are presented below.

Clearly, the positive responses for planning to continue teaching at the middle level far outweighed those given for leaving. The number of positive reasons for remaining at the middle level (746) greatly outnumbered those for not planning to stay (58). In fact, discounting the 205 neutral responses, only 58 (7%) of 804 remaining responses were negative. Perhaps these 7% are among the 13% of all the nation's teachers who plan to leave teaching when "something better comes along" or the

4% who plan to leave as soon as possible (NCES, 1993a, p. 144). It is encouraging to find that 93% of the respondents felt positive about their career choice and intended to devote their careers to teaching young adolescents.

Reasons for Continuing at the Middle Level

The reasons for continuing to teach at the middle level focused directly on enjoying/loving the age group (75% of all positive responses), the challenge and opportunity to make a positive difference in the lives of young adolescents, and clear preferences for the middle school concept, curriculum, and subject matter. Several teachers also commented about the "fit" between them and the age group. Some typical responses were:

> *I make a difference.*

> *I believe this is my 'calling.' I love this age group.*

> *I like this age group and the middle school concept.*

> *Middle school students are 'genuine' people—open, expressive, honest, friendly, and unpredictable.*

> *I love helping students through this difficult time.*

> *I have taught grades 6-8 for 25 years and intend to continue what I enjoy.*

> *Sixth graders are wonderful! This is the most exciting year. Most of the students are fresh and full of wonder and enthusiasm.*

> *The love and challenges of my seventh graders cannot be described! I can't wait to get to school every day.*

I have taught the 8th grade for 23 years. I love it!

I love the enthusiasm and spontaneity of this age group.

I feel here is where the most difference can be made. I want to be a positive influence.

Know thyself, and seventh grade is my niche!

I believe that these are the most critical years and I have a commitment to these young people.

They keep me young and laugh at my bad jokes.

Middle schoolers are a fantastic, formidable challenge.

It's where I belong.

One teacher summarized the statements of many of her colleagues when she stated: "I love what I teach, where I teach and who I teach." Another noted "P.S. There is a special place in heaven for middle school teachers!!"

Reasons For Wishing to Leave the Middle Level

It is comforting that only 58 teachers (7%) gave negative reasons for wishing to leave middle level teaching. It is a concern, however, for the young adolescents who are unfortunate enough to be assigned to them. Some sample responses were:

Too stressful—too much discipline and not enough teaching?

I have taught middle grades for 22 years, 8 more and I am out of this hell.

I am burned out. I am tired of fighting parents, students, and the system.

I find that there is a tremendous amount of baby-sitting that the middle school teacher needs to do in order to have a class run smoothly. As a result too little teaching gets done — and most of what does get done is on a basic level due to low skill ability.

It was not always clear whether respondents were negative about just the middle level, or the teaching profession in general. Seventy-four percent of the negative responses did, however, specifically focus on the difficulty of the age group and the lack of enjoyment in teaching young adolescents.

Neutral Responses

Responses that indicated reasons for leaving that were not clearly positive or negative were designated neutral. Types of such responses were: prefer working with younger children, prefer senior high school teaching, plan to become an administrator, counselor or central office curriculum supervisor. A preference for a particular age group or level was not considered inherently positive or negative, but neutral. Some specific examples follow.

I prefer to work with younger children.

I hope to receive a doctorate and teach future teachers.

I prefer the self-contained classroom.

High school students are more mature and courses are for graduation credit.

I intend to move to the high school level in order to teach physics.

I love secondary.

I am a high school varsity coach and working at the high school would be to my advantage.

I am taking a position as a pastor of middle school age students at a large church.

I am getting my masters in administration and hope to become a middle school principal.

I want to be a counselor, but would like be at the middle school level.

These last three responses are really quite positive toward the age level although our definition placed them in the neutral category.

Other Teacher Comments

A space for comments was provided at the end of the questionnaire. As would be expected, the large majority of comments focused on middle level professional preparation. Space does not allow a full reporting of these comments, however, representative sample comments are provided below.

I definitely believe middle level teacher preparation should be different from elementary and secondary. I spent my time in elementary preparation courses and learned only through experience about teaching middle school students. After 10 years of experience, I hunger for methods courses that are specifically for middle school teachers. I have had to try to learn on my own and from other teachers. ...

I have done everything possible to train myself by attending workshops and by reading. ... Perhaps the answer is train-

ing the education majors in college so they will expect no less (developmentally appropriate instruction and programs) when they arrive to teach.

Universities are taking too long in starting programs for educators dealing with this age child.

None of the classes I took focused on middle school. The focus was either elementary or secondary. I strongly believe our colleges and universities need specific preparation programs for middle school teachers.

Several teachers mentioned their concern regarding the preparation of middle school principals:

I think middle school principals should have special preparation or certification. Most teachers at my school are 'into the middle school concept,' but our current principal is not...

My primary suggestion for improvement in the middle school area would be in the area of principals. They seem to have little expertise in middle school education. ... We have had approximately 15 different principals, including assistant principals, in the last 15 years. ...

A few teachers also commented that they did not think special preparation was necessary, or that middle level preparation should be combined with elementary and/or secondary preparation.

Preparation for middle school only is not essential.

I believe good teaching spans grade levels, K-16. Methodologies are not so different that adjustments need to be made for age levels.

I think middle school education should be included in an elementary education degree. Sometimes you are not sure of which grade levels you want to teach.

The overwhelming number of comments, however, related to the importance of middle level teaching and middle level teacher preparation:

Middle level teachers should have chosen to teach the age group and specialized in order to be effective rather than be elementary/high school oriented and in middle school by default!

Being a middle level trained teacher, I am greatly concerned about the lack of training some of the more experienced teachers have. (Administrators as well). ...

Besides preparing new teachers, we need to find ways to 'convince' the experienced ones.

I hope the day comes when all middle school teachers will have to be certified specifically for middle school.

From talking with education majors who have graduated recently, a lot of the suggestions I would like to see implemented have been. They are given a much stronger background from which to work with this group of kids.

I was not prepared for a real middle school. I was prepared as an elementary teacher. Unfortunately, no one was prepared to give me a job as one. So I have been a middle school teacher for 10 years now. I am afraid I have had to learn the hard way to become a good middle school teacher (which I feel I finally am). I love my job and the children I work with, and I do not think I would be comfortable teaching at the elementary level anymore. It would have been wonderful to have been prepared back in 1982 when I started out, but I just was not. I blame that on two things: (1) I was trained to be an elementary teacher, and (2) the certificate that I received made it possible for me to teach up through eighth grade...

In summary, the tone of the open-ended section titled "comments" supported the special preparation of middle level teachers. Only four teachers noted that such preparation was probably not really needed. This last comment was typical of the many others:

I am encouraged to know that there is this interest in teacher preparation. I too believe there is definitely a need for more specific preparation for middle school teaching. This is a time of transitions in children's lives that requires understanding and techniques that consider the delicate nature of the young adolescent child. Go for it!

V.

Beyond Add-On Courses: Conclusions and Recommendations

Slightly more than half of the middle school teachers in this study had some kind of special preparation for teaching young adolescents, but the majority received it in graduate programs: just 23% received their initial professional preparation in a special middle grades program, 22% in an undergraduate program, versus 17% in the 1991 sample. Although the 1993 proportion is greater, it is still only about one in five, and given that we selected the sample to maximize that percentage, is surprisingly low.

A third of these 6th-8th grade teachers did not have special undergraduate preparation but did at the graduate level. While their eventually securing special preparation is encouraging, we also noted that these graduate-prepared teachers were no more likely to have had field experiences or student teaching at the graduate level than were graduate students in other masters or higher programs. Many graduate programs may be too brief, lasting only a year, for these experiences to be easily incorporated. Another explanation is that the graduate students have already had some years teaching before or concurrent with pursuing graduate studies, and so are not expected to participate in field experiences or student teaching at the graduate level. Also, some graduate programs require students who have not experienced middle grades field experiences and/or undergraduate preparation to take specified courses and successfully complete middle level field experiences before entering middle level graduate programs. If this is the case, then many young adolescents will be taught by teachers who eventually will get special preparation, but who do not start out with that special background.

Many middle level graduate programs also might assume that teacher candidates have the specific middle level field experiences in their undergraduate programs, an assumption that our data suggest is unwarranted. In either case, whether it is the experienced graduate student, or the graduate student pursuing advanced studies immediately after an undergraduate program, these data suggest that it is a distinct minority of middle school teachers who initially come to that task well prepared for teaching young adolescents.

Not surprisingly, teachers who had more of the seven coursework and field experience components in their professional preparation rated the quality of their preparation on middle grades issues significantly more favorably than teachers with fewer of these components, regardless of whether they were prepared in special middle grades programs or in elementary or secondary programs. Overall, however, there were some shocking gaps in the preservice preparation of those middle school teachers. More than 40% did not have coursework on how to teach young adolescents, more than half did not have coursework focusing on the curriculum and organization of the middle school, and nearly 60% did not have pre-student teaching field work or student teaching in the middle grades. Yet, they were all teaching in grades 6-8 middle schools.

The good news is that teachers who were prepared in a special middle grades program were significantly more likely to have had each of the seven types of coursework and field experience. However, teachers who had special middle-grades programs, as a whole, were only slightly more likely than other teachers to rate their programs favorably. Those with more comprehensive special middle grades programs rated their programs' coverage of middle grades content and issues significantly more favorably than those with special programs lower in comprehensiveness.

This welcome finding lends support to the belief that expanding the comprehensiveness of preservice programs preparing middle level teachers—whether they are special middle grades programs or elementary or secondary programs—will result in teachers being more adequately prepared to teach young adolescents, at least in their own eyes. It suggests that add-on courses and endorsements, while perhaps bureaucratically satisfactory shortcuts, are a less effective form of preparation for the middle grades than is a major middle grades specialization equal in scope to traditional elementary and secondary education majors.

Furthermore, on some issues it apparently is not enough to have even the majority of these coursework and fieldwork components in the program. Only those who had at least 6 or all 7 of the comprehensiveness components in their special middle grades program rated the program significantly more favorably in its coverage of cultural diversity, interdisciplinary teaming, and advisor-advisee programs. Yet these topics are among those considered most crucial for today's middle level teachers.

It is heartening that those in special middle grades preparation programs who had 6 or all 7 of the comprehensiveness components rated their coverage of cultural and language diversity more favorably than those without special preparation or with less comprehensive programs. Responding to students' cultural and language diversity clearly is not a challenge faced just by middle grades teachers but by all educators. The failure to adequately do so is not just a failure of the typical middle grades teacher preparation program, or even of the typical school of education, but of the typical university as a whole. Having a course in diversity might comply with program guidelines, but it does little to change preservice teachers' beliefs about learners' potential (Kennedy, 1991; Zeichner, 1992). Moreover, even a program that addressed diversity issues more comprehensively might leave untouched an assumption of preservice teachers that the goals of multicultural education are cooperation, tolerance, and the assimilation of minority groups, rather than promoting equality among all ethnic groups, enhancing diversity, and reconstructing society to better serve minority groups. Assimilationist goals were espoused by 66% of respondents in one study of preservice students, a result that suggests colleges must be much much more directive if they wish to change significantly "the teacher-minority student relationship as it has existed over the past twenty-five years" (Nel, 1993).

Our data do not tell us what these programs actually did that earned them more favorable ratings, but it is promising that graduates from special and highly comprehensive middle grades preparation programs evaluated their programs' coverage of diversity significantly more favorably than did graduates of other and less comprehensive preparation programs.

It is also promising that 57% of specially-prepared middle grades teachers had highly comprehensive programs. The chances that a special middle grades preparation program will be comprehensive would appear to be better than 50-50. However, just 22% of the total sample had their undergraduate preparation in special middle grades programs. Thus, just 12.5% of this large representative sample of grades 6-8 teachers had their undergraduate preparation in a highly comprehensive, special middle grades program.

The good news in this is that those middle school teachers who received their bachelors degrees in more recent years were moderately more likely to have had their initial preparation in a special middle grades program. Although the total proportion with special preparation was very much a minority, the trend seems to be that recent graduates are somewhat more likely to be specially prepared. This finding is rather in sharp contrast to the results reported by Valentine et al. (1992), who found that a much smaller proportion of teachers in 1991 than in 1982 had special university preparation for the middle level (a drop from 44% to 36%) or student teaching at the middle level (a drop from 58% to 32%). It is possible that the characteristics of responding schools contributed to the difference between our study and this NASSP-sponsored study. Valentine and associates included any grade combination between 5 and 9 while we limited our sample to grades 6-8 middle schools. Although 64% of their sample was a 6-8 or 7-8 school, the remainder were junior high schools, included grade 5, or had some other configuration, all of which would have tended to work against those teachers reporting special middle level preparation. However, the 1981 sample would have had even more of these schools, and so it is highly unlikely that a drop in preparation would be seen at the same time as observing an increase in true "middle schools."

Because there is no apparent reason for the anomalous Valentine result, we must surmise that the principals' impressions of teachers' preparation were simply inaccurate. Our data came from teachers themselves reporting about their own preparation.

Finally, we reported that teachers who held an authentic middle level certificate were significantly more likely to have had comprehensive programs and to rate those programs more favorably than teachers whose certificates were not as authentically focused on the middle level. This finding too suggests that states that solely utilize overlapping certificates to cover the middle grades are likely to be states whose teacher graduates have less comprehensive middle grades programs that they view as inadequately preparing them to teach young adolescents. Although cause and effect cannot be determined from the data, it is highly unlikely that colleges adopt comprehensive programs and that these in turn cause a state to offer an authentic, minimally overlapping middle level certificate. More likely is that a state framework that includes an authentic middle level certificate encourages preparation program comprehensiveness, which in turn is associated with more favorable teacher evaluations of the quality of their preparation.

The challenge to teacher educators is clear. Across the total sample and also among the teachers prepared in special middle grades programs, even the group with the most comprehensive programs gave mean program ratings on nearly all topics indicating they had been prepared just "adequately" rather than "very well." And as was discovered in the 1991 study, even teachers with highly comprehensive programs veered too close to the "inadequate" mark for most educators' comfort on preparation for dealing with cultural diversity, and readiness to participate in teacher-based guidance programs and interdisciplinary teaming.

These data suggest that far more middle grades teachers need to be specially-prepared in highly comprehensive middle grades programs, and that even highly comprehensive special middle grades programs, while clearly better than less comprehensive programs, must improve in other ways if they are to be excellent and not just adequate.

These responses might be tapping the difference between various perspectives on the curriculum. The *formal* curriculum is reflected in the course syllabus, the *perceived* curriculum represents what faculty think is important to emphasize, the *operational* curriculum is what the professor actually teaches, and the *experiential* curriculum is what the student perceives to be happening (Edmundson, 1989). For example, the National Middle School Association/National Council for Accreditation of Teacher Education Curriculum Guidelines call for an "identifiable program" of middle level education. A special track with only a few courses might satisfy that formal requirement. Offering a comprehensive program including special courses on middle level learners, curriculum, and organization and requiring middle level field experiences is a better choice and will yield more positive results. College faculty modelling an interdisciplinary approach (not just having readings about it), doing so teamed with middle school teachers, and having preservice teachers team with each other to develop integrative curriculum is a more substantial effort to achieve excellence by actually having the formal, perceived, operational, and experiential curricula be in tune with each other.

Moreover, even programs that boast all the coursework and fieldwork components we examined (the formal curriculum) and emphasized the topics teachers say most need emphasis (the perceived curriculum) could be rated unfavorably if they used ineffective instructional practices (the operational and experiential curriculum). In the Study of the Education of Educators, for example, students reported that faculty demonstration, discussion, and feedback were employed by 40% or fewer of professors in educational foundations and psychology courses (Soder, 1989). Although these approaches were used much more in methods courses, as one would expect, there were still some large gaps between how much students hoped these active methods would be used and how much they perceived them being used.

Newmann and Wehlage (1993) carried this reasoning farther in their description of what constitutes "authentic instruction." They noted that even active approaches, including cooperative learning or on-the-job apprenticeships, can fail to produce authentic achievement if poorly implemented. They described five standards of authentic instruction that were derived from the experience of schools trying to restructure, but that seem to be equally useful as guideposts for examining preservice programs. In the Newmann and Wehlage framework, authentic instruction occurs when:

1. student use of higher-order thinking is central;
2. student knowledge is deep;
3. students are connected to the world beyond the classroom;
4. students engage in substantive conversation in unscripted exchanges with each other and with faculty; and,
5. the teacher conveys social support for student achievement, including high expectations for all students and an environment of mutual respect in which taking intellectual risks is encouraged.

Although Newmann and Wehlage referred to pre-collegiate schooling, these are substantial dimensions of authenticity that most middle grades teachers have not experienced in their preservice preparation. Little (1993) got at another missing element, that is, the ability of teachers to "act as shapers, promoters, and critics" of school reform. Her discussion focused more on the continuing education of teachers but also was relevant to preservice program quality. Little noted that the conventional preparation and coaching model of professional teacher development does little to expand teachers' notions of their possibilities.

Central to these broadened possibilities, she believes, is for teachers (and we add preservice teachers) "to contend with fundamental debates and disagreements about the purposes of schooling, the relationships between teachers and students, and the obligations of teachers to the wider larger community . . .," an experience that is impossible unless the school (or teacher education program) has a "tolerance for public dispute over fundamental matters" (p. 140).

Sarason (1993) also wrote that teacher education students generally have limited knowledge about how and why schools are organized the way they are, obstacles to change, how non-teaching personnel affect the system, power and decision-making issues, in short, "almost all the factors that will impinge on them, shape them as persons and professionals, determine their self-esteem or personal worth, and stimulate or inhibit their creativity and professional growth" (p. 115). He proposed a year-long *Culture of Schools* field experience involving not just classroom experiences, but considerable time spent with non-teaching personnel from school nurses to the superintendent, school board meetings, collective bargaining meetings, and education seminars by anthropologists, psychologists, sociologists, political scientists, economists, and historians.

Relevant here is a promising finding from another Center for Early Adolescence study of 175 middle-grades teacher educators (Scales, in press). In that study, education deans and directors at the nations's 241 middle grades teacher preparation programs were asked to request faculty who regularly taught middle grades foundations, psychology, or methods courses, or who supervised field experiences, to complete a questionnaire on the resources they used or wished to have in their programs, and on their views about ways to strengthen their programs. A response rate of 51% was achieved with 175 faculty responses coming from 124 institutions. These professors recommended that college faculty model more the teaching techniques they hope students will learn, and collaborate more, on-site, with middle school teachers. The recommendations middle school teachers are making to improve preservice preparation are not in conflict with teacher educators' hopes. If state policymakers and college administrators make the resources available and the regulatory environment supportive of comprehensive, special middle grades programs, there is no reason to doubt that school and college educators together can greatly strengthen the way middle grades teachers are prepared.

An Agenda for Excellence in Middle Grades Teacher Education

Combining the results of the present study with the results of the expert Delphi (discussed in Section Two) and the other two Center for Early Adolescence studies of middle grades teacher educators and middle grades teachers (Scales, in press; Scales, 1992a), we conclude that the following are the consensus recommendations of middle grades teachers, teacher educators, and early adolescence experts.

To attain excellence, middle grades teacher education programs should:

1. be conducted at the school site as much as possible and involve considerable collaboration between middle schools and universities (with teachers providing continuing education for college faculty, with co-designed and co-taught courses) and within universities, (across schools and departments);
2. be staffed with faculty who model the techniques they expect preservice teachers to learn, especially interdisciplinary/integrative curriculum, cooperative learning, teacher-based guidance/advisor-advisee; and portfolio/exhibition assessment approaches;

3. provide resources for ongoing faculty development, including regular contact with and teaching young adolescents;
4. enable their students to engage in fieldwork in the first and second years of an undergraduate program;
5. ensure that students' fieldwork includes a variety of community settings that young adolescents use or frequent;
6. maintain a core library of resources teacher educators considered essential for middle grades teacher preparation;
7. provide faculty and students with experiences of systems responding to young adolescents' characteristics, both communities/neighborhoods and restructuring schools;
8. provide extensive student experiences in how to involve families and community resources with middle schools;
9. include extensive opportunities to learn about being an advisor in a teacher-based guidance program; interdisciplinary teaming; responding to students' cultural and language diversity; and,
10. ensure that students acquire a comprehensive understanding of young adolescent social relationships and self-awareness concerns, especially health and sexuality.

Taken together, these recommendations call for a drastic change in the way middle grades teacher preparation programs are structured. The essential change is that of self-perception and self-definition on the part of university teacher educators. Instead of the university campus being an island on which students reside except for brief "field experiences" in mainland schools, a bridge should be built between the two institutions to promote ongoing, continuous collaboration and exchange. The key requirement for building these bridges is the perception that teachers are the professional equals of teacher educators, a perception that often has run counter to the prevailing university emphasis on research and scholarship as the hallmarks of professionalism (Goodlad, 1990).

Our study of middle grades teacher educators, however, suggests that university teacher educators are eager to learn from their school-based colleagues (Scales, in press). In the Center for Early Adolescence "Building Bridges" project with three university-school partnerships, both the University of New Mexico and Southern Illinois University-Edwardsville now include university faculty based either half-time or full-time at their partner middle schools (Johnson and North middle schools, respectively). Although only the first step toward becoming full-fledged professional development schools (Lieberman & Miller, 1990; Nystrand, 1991), the occupying of physical space in the middle school by the university teacher preparation program does a great deal to create a sense that the teacher education program is becoming a joint endeavor of the two institutions. An extension of the professional development school model is occurring in Detroit, where Wayne State University has opened a public middle school in which university students and professors from a variety of disciplines are expected to be heavily involved, with an emphasis on providing a full range of educational and health services for students and a research and training environment for student teachers and experienced educators (Bradley, 1993).

An important component of the increased site-based structure of teacher preparation programs is that teacher educators get to interact more with young adolescents than they normally might. Our studies suggest that middle grades teacher educators have been too long apart from middle grades students: Nearly three-fourths of one sample had most recently taught in the middle grades more than seven years ago (Scales, in press). Approaches such as San Francisco State University's requirement that teacher educators take a semester off every few years to teach in K-12 schools are "far from widespread" (Olsen & Mellen, 1990), but might be one of the components middle grades teacher preparation programs need to build in to help keep college faculty current and to strengthen the collaboration bond between college and middle school faculty.

The respondents in our several studies made it clear that in addition to personally working with young adolescents and being committed to university-school partnerships, successful middle grades teachers need to know how students' families affect their learning, and how teachers and schools can enhance family participation in students' learning (Davies, 1991). Moreover, the young adolescents who are at home and in school classrooms for part of the day are for the rest of the day in playgrounds and on the streets, in youth groups, religious organizations, neighborhood libraries, children's museums, work settings, health clinics, and organized after-school programs. Teachers who interact with young adolescents in these other settings gain a rich appreciation for the total environment in which young adolescents develop.

Bucci and Reitzammer (1992) recommend that preservice teachers have a "short field placement or shadowing experience" in such settings. Those who do will get to learn vicariously about the "multiple me's" (Harter, 1990) that comprise young adolescents' search for a coherent identity. They may see talents and interests displayed that are hidden in a school setting and feel some of the pressures that young adolescents face out of school that affect their work in school. Because young adolescents' physical, cognitive, and socio-emotional development is so intimately connected, those helpers and educators who see only a piece of development have limited potential effectiveness.

Interacting with young adolescents, and in more varied settings than just schools, can have another benefit for preservice students. Although one of the core issues driving school restructuring is to equalize the learning opportunities of advantaged and disadvantaged students, attention to "at-risk" youth can have the deleterious effect of focusing educators and helpers on students' deficits rather than on their assets or strengths. The wider the variety of settings in which preservice teachers see young adolescents, especially young adolescents living in poverty, the more likely it is that they will be able to see beyond the obvious challenges in these young peoples' lives and perceive as well the personal, family, and community assets that most of those "at-risk" youth also possess. Such exposure may help raise new teachers' expectations about what these young adolescents can actually achieve, and so, in turn, lead to providing a more challenging curriculum. For example, Goucher College buttresses such varied field settings with courses, not just on the "at-risk" student, but, unusually, on the resilient student and the concept of social, educational, and familial protective factors and competencies (*Master of Education Program, 1992*).

Enabling preservice middle grades teachers to have field experiences in a variety of community-based settings is most likely if the university-school partnership concurs with the Council of Chief State School Officers' recommendation that "every community should develop a school-linked support system for children and their families" (*Student Success ..., 1992*). In a community where various institutions are committed to this unifying principle of creating, not just a responsive school, but a responsive ecology for young adolescents, a next logical step beyond placing student teachers in community-based field settings is constructing a system in which preservice practitioners from a variety of disciplines are prepared together.

One of the few examples of such an innovation is the University of Washington's "Training for Interprofessional Collaboration." As part of their Carnegie Corporation-sponsored middle grades reform activities, the University's College of Education, Graduate School of Public Affairs, and Schools of Social Work, Nursing and Public Health, and Community Medicine joined forces to develop eight service delivery sites that integrate these disciplines and the services they provide, as well as develop interprofessional curriculum and field experiences. One of the first two sites is a middle school in downtown Seattle, served by the TIC program and a collaborative network of ten youth agencies. School staff and agency staff are trained and integrated into the supervision of the University's preservice students as they go through their field placements (*Training for Interprofessional Collaboration, 1992*).

A corollary to the necessary greater sense of professional equality between teachers and teacher educators is a greater felt need to immerse, not just expose, preservice students early on in their preparation to successful, restructured middle schools. Traditionally, field experiences begin in the third or fourth year of an undergraduate program, and the results of our several studies suggest that middle grades teachers and teacher educators alike agree that the first and second years are not too early for working in the field. Middle level teacher educators rate highly the goal of helping preservice teachers deepen their understanding of systemic school change (Scales, in press) and it is doubtful that such understanding can be achieved without considerable personal experience in such schools.

One program that is touted as one of the nation's best examples of "full-scale integration of teacher education into the public schools," the Southern Maine Partnership that links the University of Southern Maine with a network of Coalition of Essential Schools members, goes so far as to limit teacher education only to schools that are restructuring: "That means no part of the agenda — new teacher preparation, teacher development in the schools, and school renewal — takes place in isolation" (Cushman, 1993).

Moreover, our respondents note that preservice students must personally experience what it is they are expected to do when they work with young adolescents. Does one truly understand cooperative learning strategies if one only reads about them? If the teacher preparation program is structured by disciplines, how effectively can that prepare preservice teachers for interdisciplinary, theme-oriented teaching? If university faculty are themselves largely distant from the personal lives and concerns of their education students, how readily will those preservice teachers take on the responsibility of being an advisor to middle grades students? Awareness that middle grades teacher preparation programs have not prepared students well to assume these roles and responsibilities has led more programs to focus on modelling the practices they want preservice teachers to implement.

For example, at Ohio State University, cohorts of preservice middle grades teachers are formed into four-person teams for a five-quarter hour program called Teaching Early Adolescents in Middle Schools (TEAMS). The teams are mentored not by individual cooperating teachers, but by entire school interdisciplinary teams as they develop and teach interdisciplinary lessons across mathematics, sciences, language arts, and social studies (Cunningham and Shillington, 1990). Middle schools also increasingly are providing service learning opportunities for young adolescents, and universities in several states are beginning to incorporate service learning experiences into their preservice programs as a result of an initiative sponsored by the DeWitt Wallace-Reader's Digest Fund. Mississippi State University, for example, has decided to link student teaching placements with local schools that get grants under the National and Community Service Act, and to develop a training program to encourage teacher educators to become personally involved in service learning (Allam & Zerkin, 1993).

All of the Center for Early Adolescence university-school partnerships (University of New Mexico-Johnson Middle School, Southern Illinois University at Edwardsville-North Middle School, and Mesa State College (CO)-Redlands Middle School) have adopted the goal of modelling what they expect preservice teachers to do as part of their initiatives for strengthening their middle grades preparation programs. They understand that, as the Goddard College (VT) Program in Middle Level Education puts it, "our students (will be) prepared to facilitate this sort of learning experience for others in part because they have experienced it themselves" (*Program In Middle Level Education, 1993*). Incorporating such changes is not simple or inexpensive. Drexel University, for example, is re-tooling its entire undergraduate curriculum in engineering, arts and sciences, business, design, and information studies to be based on interdisciplinary studies, a move it estimates will cost about 10% more than its traditional, separate discipline approach (Collison, 1993).

We have discussed most of these recommendations before, but one more deserves additional comment. Many of our respondent teachers, in their extended written remarks, referred to the importance of understanding young adolescent health issues, from nutrition and fitness, to guns at school and conflict resolution, mental health, and sexuality. Threats to health and well-being increase during early adolescence, as young people begin making life-style choices that can either increase or decrease their risks. For example, 40% of young adolescents have had sexual intercourse at least once by the age of 15, according to the Centers for Disease Control (Sexual Behavior..., 1992) and most have had their initial experience with cigarettes and alcohol by the end of early adolescence (Scales, 1991). Most critically, early adolescence is, after all, the stage during which puberty occurs and so it is the stage during which sex-related concerns become significantly more important. No thorough understanding of young adolescent development can be complete without a deep understanding of early adolescent health, especially young adolescents' sexual development and need for comprehensive sexuality education.

The National Middle School Association/National Council for Accreditation of Teacher Education-Approved Curriculum Guidelines for middle level teacher preparation programs do not place a special emphasis upon health and sexuality in early adolescence as important components of a good preparation program, but that lack of emphasis might soon be changing. The National Board for Professional Teaching Standards developed standards for certification as an Early Adolescent/Generalist, and recommended that all teachers of young adolescents have a solid background in six core areas, one of which was health.

The inclusion of health (and the arts) along with the usual "big four" (language arts, social studies, sciences, and mathematics) represents a significant change in conceptualizing what a typical teacher of young adolescents should know. Most middle grades teacher preparation programs that want to prepare excellent middle school teachers will need to increase their emphasis upon health and sexuality issues to enable their graduates to meet this more comprehensive standard.

Health education can link content disciplines that are especially important to young adolescents, and is one of the best vehicles for promoting young adolescent critical thinking (Scales, 1993) because it is a discipline in which so many young adolescent personal concerns and social issues intersect. These intersections are considered to be the fundamental building blocks of effective middle school curriculum (Beane, 1993). The Sex Information and Education Council of the United States has produced a carefully delineated set of guidelines for comprehensive sexuality education, organized by learners' developmental levels (Guidelines, ..., 1992), and the Association for the Advancement of Health Education is developing national standards for K-12 health education more broadly. Although we think all early adolescence generalists need not be certified in health education, preservice preparation programs that want to provide a truly thorough grounding in these critical young adolescent issues should ensure that preservice students understand much that is contained in these emerging health and sexuality education guidelines.

Clearly, there are other actions that can be taken to improve middle grades teacher preparation programs. But two seem to be the most critical: (1) states should require a separate certification for the middle level, thereby ensuring the comprehensive program that our results show is strongly associated with teachers feeling well-prepared, and (2) those programs should implement the ten recommendations we have presented. If those two steps were taken, we believe the next generation of middle grades teacher preparation programs would be far superior to the typical programs students experience today. Graduates from such programs would feel ready, and arguably be ready, to provide a diverse young adolescent population with challenging and developmentally-responsive curriculum and instruction, and to themselves actively respond to changing social realities.

And as the middle school concept becomes more fully operational the demands that teachers be broadly prepared, comfortable on a team, and able to serve as an advisor or advocate will increase. Specialized and distinctive teacher preparation will be even more critical than it is today. While growing pains are accepted as a reality, teacher educators must become much more aggressive in efforts to establish the middle level certification and teacher preparation programs needed.

Limitations of This Study

No study is without qualifications, and there are several limitations to our study that should be kept in mind. First, slightly more than half (52%) of the original sample of all 1,100 middle schools in the five states returned no teacher questionnaires. Our school and teacher response rates of 48% and 79%, respectively, were substantially higher than the Center's earlier study (Scales, 1992a), but it is possible that non-respondents differed from respondents on key characteristics. However, Scales selected that earlier sample not by school, but by teacher's grade taught and type of community (rural, urban, suburban) and reported no significant differences between respondents and non-respondents on these stratification variables. We have no reason to suspect any different a response from the 1993 sample.

Because the 1993 sample was selected to have even less variation in grades and building configurations than the 1991 sample, we believe these variables would be associated with no more and probably less impact on our dependent variables than reported in Scales' 1992 study. Clearly, the recollections of comprehensiveness and, perhaps especially, the teachers' subjective ratings of preparation program adequacy, could have been differentially affected by other variables about which we have no information to distinguish a possible respondent-non-respondent difference. However, it seems most likely to us that non-respondents would be less likely to have had special preparation. We see no apparent reason why these non-respondents' recollections of program comprehensiveness or ratings of program adequacy would be in a distribution markedly different from those nearly 1,000 teachers who did not have special preparation at either the undergraduate or graduate level. If that is the case, then, if anything we have underestimated the positive impact of having had special preparation. Adding in those non-respondents would make the observed differences stronger, not weaker.

Second, a different and more crucial limitation to this study, and to all other research to date on the impact of preparing middle grades teachers, is that our data are teachers' self-reports. Although the consistency of the results, both within this study and the similarity of the results with the Scales 1992 study lead us to have confidence in the reliability of most of the data (with the exception of semester hours teachers say they had in their programs), the question of validity remains.

One of our key dependent variables, the teachers' ratings of their preparation program adequacy, is a subjective, retrospective rating. Would ratings of new graduates or first-year teachers be the same as those obtained from this sample where nearly half had been teaching 10 years or more? We suspect the new graduates' ratings would be more positive, and that their evaluation of their preparation would become less favorable as their experience increased, but we have no data with which to investigate that possibility, and to guess by how much those ratings would decline is even more an exercise in speculation.

Furthermore, what is the association between teachers' ratings of their preparation program, their recollections of its comprehensiveness, and their actual teaching behaviors, at whatever stage of their career the data are collected? The literature does not yet tell us whether teachers who went through a special middle grades program, especially one that was highly comprehensive and that they rated favorably, actually exhibit and use more than other middle grades teachers the curriculum, teaching, and classroom management techniques they remember so positively. We need to know whether they do, not just by teacher self-reports, but through observation (video, journaling, teacher/principal observations) or young adolescent student reports.

It seems logical to assume that teachers who had such a special, comprehensive background that they recall so favorably would in fact be more likely than teachers without such a background to effectively use the techniques and skills they were taught. But the literature is also filled with compelling evidence that the culture of the school experienced while actually teaching as a certified teacher and not a student teacher exerts a powerful influence on the great majority of neophyte teachers, causing most to adopt the norms and cultural folkways of their school, even at the expense of what they learned was the "right" thing to do in college or graduate school. The answers to these questions await future research.

The Critical Issue of Preparing the Teachers of Teachers

This study does not address the question of how the teachers of future middle grades teachers are being prepared. This could be considered a limitation. What special preparation do middle grades teacher educators receive, and how well does that prepare them to help preservice students become excellent middle school teachers? These are questions that need to be addressed.

The number of middle-grades teacher educators across the nation is small — in Scales 1992 study, it was reported that 70% of education deans and directors in eight states said there were just two to five people knowledgeable about and active in middle grades education on their faculties/staffs. If those figures hold throughout the nation's approximately 241 institutions with middle grades teacher preparation programs, which is highly unlikely, then there are at best just 600 to 800 teacher educators in the entire country specializing in the middle level.

Another Center study (Scales, in press) provided some information about 175 of these teacher educators. Nearly all were white, evenly split between men and women, and the majority had taught in grades 5-9, especially in grades 6-8. More than one-quarter had taught within the middle grades during the previous seven years, but the vast majority held a non-authentic certificate that ended in grade 12, not an authentic certificate focused on the middle grades. Sixty percent had been a teacher educator for 11 years or more. Given how long ago they received their preparation, it seems almost certain that the majority of the nation's middle grades teacher educators themselves did not receive special preservice preparation for teaching young adolescents, but rather acquired their training on the job and in subsequent formal graduate schooling after their initial teaching experiences. Our knowledge of their specific preparation for teaching future middle school teachers is scant. Yet, if middle grades teacher preparation programs are to continue to improve, attention must also be paid to how the teachers of teachers are prepared.

This is especially true if one of the aspects of program improvement is greater collaboration and a different kind of more equal partnership between middle schools and university preparation programs. To emphasize this dimension of strengthening middle grades preparation programs means to be concerned not just with the quality of the preservice preparation that student teachers receive, but also with the kind of continuing education and professional development that teacher educators and cooperating teachers experience.

Some Final Thoughts

Results from this study provide clear directions for those responsible for the professional preparation of middle level teachers as they make decisions regarding program design and related matters. Much more is now known about what practicing middle school teachers believe constitutes a quality middle grades teacher preparation program. The collective insights of these 2,139 teachers offer valuable information concerning essential program components, levels of specialized program comprehensiveness, and other important programmatic considerations. This study also includes strong messages for policymakers regarding practices which promote or thwart the effective preparation of prospective and practicing middle grades teachers. This is especially important when one considers that the results, even from the five states that contain over one-half of the nation's specialized middle level teacher preparation programs and have distinctive certification, show that almost half of the teachers teaching young adolescents in those states have had no special preparation to do so. Results also revealed that even in comprehensive programs, gaps are present that need to be filled if quality middle level teacher preparation is to become widely available.

Several key findings and some final thoughts are presented here. This is not intended to be a comprehensive summary of the several studies reported in *Growing Pains,* but rather only a restatement of some selected points appropriate in this concluding section. Many other findings, recommendations found elsewhere in this book and related discussions, particularly the ten major recommendations on pages 60-61, hold important implications for middle level teacher preparation and must receive careful consideration.

The Extent of Specialized Middle Grades Preparation

- Only 23 percent of the teachers surveyed in these five states that had separate and distinct middle level certification had received their initial teacher preparation in a middle level teacher preparation program.
- Only 22 percent of them had received undergraduate preparation in a program specifically designed for middle grades teaching.
- Recently graduated middle school teachers were moderately more likely to have received specialized middle level preparation.
- Fifty-seven percent of teachers with special preparation were graduates of highly comprehensive programs.
- Sixty-seven percent of those with graduate degrees (56%) indicated that their most recent preparation was for middle level teaching.
- Approximately 55% (22% initial and 33% graduate) of all respondents had some kind of middle level preparation while nearly half had no special preparation.

These and related findings are discouraging, although progress is being made in these five states where a commitment has been made to encourage, and in some cases require, that teachers of young adolescents receive special middle grades professional preparation. For example, certification requirements in North Carolina meet and exceed the National Middle School Association/National Council for Accreditation of Teacher Education-Approved Curriculum Guidelines. Mandatory middle grades certification in North Carolina has resulted in Middle Grades Education becoming a "third level" of teacher preparation focusing on the specialized knowledge and skills needed for successful middle level teaching. Such actions in the five states selected for this study have resulted in the bare majority of middle school teachers in these states (55%) having received special middle grades preparation at some degree level. And this percentage is likely to increase significantly over the next several years as larger numbers of teachers gain access to these specialized preparation programs. But what of the other 45 states with less specific certification requirements?

It should be recognized that this study presents a "best-case scenario" in another respect, since responding teachers were teaching in middle schools, the grade organization where the largest number of specially prepared teachers are found. This means that even fewer classrooms in schools with other grade organizations but which enroll young adolescents have specially prepared middle grades teachers.

In summary, much progress has been made in some states, yet so much remains to be accomplished. This is especially true in those many states that have not yet initiated efforts to ensure that teachers of young adolescents have any special middle level professional preparation.

The Comprehensiveness of Specialized Middle Level Teacher Preparation Programs.

- Teachers prepared in special middle grades programs were more likely to have had each of the seven program components considered essential for teaching successfully at the middle grades level.
- The more middle level courses preservice teachers take, the more likely they are to report their program was highly comprehensive. The greater the number of courses devoted to the middle level, the more favorably respondents rated their middle level preparation programs on each of the topics investigated.

- When the total sample was considered, respondents with special middle level preparation were only somewhat more likely than those without it to rate their preparation programs highly. However, those who had been prepared in highly comprehensive, special middle grades programs gave more favorable ratings to their programs, on each topic, than teachers who had been prepared in programs with medium or low comprehensiveness.
- Teachers who were graduates of comprehensive middle grades preparation programs were more likely to rate their programs favorably in the areas of cultural and language diversity than were those with less comprehensive programs.
- The divided group, e.g. elementary/middle, middle/secondary, was not significantly more likely that the non-focused, e.g. grades K-12 elementary/middle/secondary, group to have had any of the seven program comprehensiveness components.

These and related findings revealed that respondents from comprehensive middle grades preparation programs, those including six or seven of the essential program components, rated their preparation much more positively that those who attended programs that were less comprehensive (five or fewer of the essential components). An important key message from these teachers was that a "few courses" added to an existing major and/or "endorsement only" programs are not adequate. Comprehensive, carefully planned preparation programs which focus exclusively on teaching young adolescents are needed.

Certification/Licensure and Specialized Preparation

- Nearly half of the sample (49%) listed as their first certificate an "authentic" middle level certificate, one that did not include large overlaps into elementary or secondary grades, e.g. 4-8, 6-9.
- Those who had authentic middle level preparation were more likely to have had special middle level preparation and to have been in comprehensive programs, and, if their programs were highly comprehensive, were more likely to give favorable ratings to their programs' coverage of the seven topics considered crucial for effective middle level teaching.
- The divided group was not significantly more likely than non-focused group to have any of the seven program comprehensiveness components. The non-focused group was significantly more likely than the divided group to have "coursework focusing on teaching reading at the middle level."
- Teachers who held an authentic middle level certificate were significantly more likely to have had comprehensive programs and to rate those programs more favorably than teachers whose certificates were not as authentically focused on the middle level.

Results from this study indicate that add-on courses and endorsements, while perhaps bureaucratically satisfactory short-cuts, are simply a less effective form of preparation than a major comprehensive program. States that use overlapping certificates that cover middle grades are likely to be states whose teacher graduates have less comprehensive middle grades programs, and view those programs as inadequately preparing them to teach young adolescents. It is also likely that a state framework that includes an authentic middle level certificate encourages preparation program comprehensiveness, which in turn is associated with teachers giving more favorableevaluations of their preparation. The cumulative wisdom of decades of experience which is reflected in the data reported here indicate that states should require a separate certification/license for middle grades teachers. This is necessary to ensure the existence of a comprehensive program that this study shows is strongly associated with teachers feeling well-prepared for guiding young adolescents.

Gaps Between Current Practices and Highly Effective Programs

- Fifty percent of the respondents rated as inadequate or poor their preparation on seven topics considered to be essential for middle grades teacher preparation programs. These topics included interdisciplinary teaming and teacher-based guidance, two topics of great importance at the middle level.
- More than 40% of the teachers that had received some level of special middle level preparation did not have coursework on teaching young adolescents, more than one-half did not have coursework focusing on curriculum and organization of the middle school, and nearly 60% did not have pre-student teaching field work or student teaching in the middle grades.
- Since many middle level teachers who receive special middle level preparation do not do so until graduate school, many thousands of middle school classrooms are staffed with teachers with no specialized middle level professional preparation. When this situation is added to the fact that only 22% of the teachers responding to this survey indi-

cated that they received special middle grades preparation before beginning their teaching career, it is clear that even in these five states where middle level teacher preparation is a priority, much additional improvement is needed.

- Teachers in more comprehensive programs gave mean ratings of "adequate" rather than "very well" on most topics. Even in these highly comprehensive programs, the ratings were too often close to the "inadequate mark" when dealing with topics such as cultural diversity, and readiness to participate in teacher-based guidance and interdisciplinary teaming.

Far more middle grades teachers need to be prepared in highly comprehensive programs, and even highly comprehensive programs must improve in other ways if they are to be excellent and not just "adequate." All those responsible for the professional preparation of middle grades teachers, not just teacher preparation personnel, need to make concerted efforts to "turn the corner" on this long needed reform and often debated issue of specialized middle level teacher preparation. The 2,139 practicing professionals who participated in this study have helped us focus on directions that need to be taken in this effort.

Concluding Statements

Middle grades preservice teachers, cooperating teachers, and teacher educators comprise a system trying to become more effectively coordinated than ever before. As it develops, the system reveals both its growing pains and its promise. Development, whether of the young adolescent or of the teachers of those young adolescents, is not without its challenges, risks, setbacks, losses, and failures. But out of those adolescent growing pains, with the right kind of knowledge, skills, and support, can emerge a healthy, happy, and productive adult. If middle grades teacher educators and policymakers approach the task of program development with the same optimism, openness, and energy as most young adolescents do, those institutional growing pains also will pay off. Through that difficult growth, a generation of comprehensively prepared teachers will emerge, teachers who feel they have been given an excellent start and the promise of continuing support so that they can really make a positive difference in the lives of the young adolescents that teach. Our teachers and our youth deserve no less.

References

Alexander, W. M., & McEwin, C. K. (1989). *Schools in the middle: Status and progress.* Columbus, OH: National Middle School Association.

Alexander, W. M., & McEwin, C. K. (1988). *Preparing to teach at the middle level.* Columbus, OH: National Middle School Association.

Allam, C., & Zerkin, B. (1993). The case for integrating service-learning into teacher preparation programs. *The Generator,* (newsletter of National Youth Leadership Council) *13*(1), 11-13.

Beane, J. (1993). *A middle school curriculum: From rhetoric to reality.* Columbus, OH: National Middle School Association.

Bradley, A. (1993, April 28). University in Detroit to open public middle school in fall. *Education Week, 12*(31).

Bucci, J. A., and Reitzammer, A. F. (1992). Collaboration with health and social service professionals: Preparing teachers for new roles. *Journal of Teacher Education, 43*(4), 290-295.

Collison, M. N-K. (1993, November 10). Learning communities for all. *Chronicle of Higher Education, 40*(12), A18.

Cunningham, R. C., & Shillington, N. M. (1990). Mentoring preservice teachers through interdisciplinary teams: A school-university partnership. *Action in Teacher Education, 11*(4), 6-11.

Cushman, K. (1993). Teacher education in essential schools: The university- school partnership, *Horace (Coalition of Essential Schools Newsletter), 10*(1), 1-8.

Davies, D. (1991). Schools reaching out: Family, school, and community partnerships for student success, *Phi Delta Kappan, 72*(5), 376-382.

Edmundson, P. J. (1989, August). *The curriculum in teacher education.* Seattle: Center for Educational Renewal, University of Washington, Technical Report No. 6.

Epstein, J. L., & Mac Iver, D. (1990). *Education in the middle grades: National practices and trends.* Columbus, Ohio: National Middle School Association.

Goodlad, J. I. (1990). *Teachers for our nation's schools.* San Francisco: Jossey-Bass.

Guidelines for comprehensive sexuality education, kindergarten through 12th grade (1992). NY: Sex Information and Education Council of the United States.

Harter, S. (1990). Processes underlying adolescent self-concept formation. In Montemayor, R., Adams, G. R, & Gullotta, T. P (Eds.), *From childhood to adolescence: A transitional period?* Newbury Park, CA: Sage, 205-239.

Kennedy, M. M. (1991). Some surprising findings on how teachers learn to teach. *Educational Leadership, 49*(3), 14-17.

Lieberman, A., & Miller, L. (1990). Teacher development in professional practice schools, *Teachers College Record 92*(1), 105-122.

Little, J. W. (1993, Summer). Teachers' professional development in a climate of educational reform. *Educational Evaluation and Policy Analysis, 15*(2), 129-151.

Master of education program catalog (1992). Baltimore, MD: Goucher College, Sheppard Pratt National Center for Human Development.

McEwin, C. K., & Dickinson, T. S. (in press). *The professional preparation of middle level teachers.* Columbus, OH: National Middle School Association.

McEwin, C. K., & Dickinson, T. S., & Jenkins, D. M. Working paper from: *The middle school after 25 years: A national status report on programs and practices.* Columbus, OH: National Middle School Association.

National Center for Educational Statistics (1993a). *America's teachers: Profile of a profession.* Washington, D.C: Office of Educational Research and Improvement.

National Center for Educational Statistics (1993b). *Schools and staffing in the United States: A statistical profile.* Washington, D.C: Office of Educational Research and Improvement.

Nel, J. (1993). Preservice teachers' perceptions of the goals of multicultural education: Implications for the empowerment of minority students, *Educational Horizons 71*(3), 120-125.

Newmann, F. M. & Whelage, G. G. (1991, Spring). Standards of authentic instruction, *Issues in restructuring schools,* No. 4, Madison, WI: Center on Organization and Restructuring of Schools, University of Wisconsin.

Nystrand, R. O. (1991). Professional development schools: toward a new relationship for schools and universities. Washington, DC: *ERIC Clearinghouse on Teacher Education,* American Association of Colleges for Teacher Education.

Olsen, L, & Mullen, N. A. (1990). *Embracing diversity: teachers' voices from California's classrooms.* San Francisco: California Tomorrow Immigrant Students Project.

Page, F. M., Page, J. A., & Dickinson, T. S. (1992). 4000 Voices. *Middle School Journal, 24*(1), 1-12.

Program in Middle Level Education (1993). Plainfield, VT: Goddard College.

Sarason, S. B. (1993). *The case for change: Rethinking the preparation of educators.* San Francsico: Jossey-Bass.

Scales, P. C. (in press). A survey of U.S. middle-grades teacher educators: Resources and recommendations for strengthening university teacher preparation programs. *Middle School Journal.*

Scales, P. C. (1993). The centrality of health education to developing young adolescents' critical thinking, *Journal of Health Education 24*(6), S10-S14.

Scales, P. C. (1993). How teachers and deans rate the quality of teacher preparation for the middle grades, *Journal of Teacher Education, 44*(5), 378-383.

Scales, P. C. (1992a). *Windows of opportunity: Improving middle grades teacher preparation.* Carrboro, NC: Center for Early Adolescence, University of North Carolina at Chapel Hill.

Scales, P. C., (1992b). The effect of preservice preparation on middle grades teachers' beliefs about teaching and teacher education, *Midpoints, 2(*2), Columbus OH: National Middle School Association.

Scales, P. C. (1991). *A portrait of young adolescents in the 1990s: Implications for promoting healthy growth and development.* Carrboro, NC: Center for Early Adolescence, University of North Carolina at Chapel Hill.

Sexual behavior among high school students—United States (1990). *Morbidity and Mortality Weekly Report, 51/52,* 885-888.

Soder, R. (1989). *Students and faculty in teacher education. Seattle:* Center for Educational Renewal, University of Washington, Technical Report #8.

Student success through collaboration: A policy statement (1992). Washington, DC: Council of Chief State School Officers.

Training for interprofessional collaboration, Fact sheet, (1992). Seattle: University of Washington, Human Service Policy Center.

Valentine, J. W., Clark, D. C. Irwin, J. L. Keefe, J. W. & Melton, G. (1993). *Leadership in middle level education: A national survey of middle level leaders and schools.* Volume I, Reston, VA: National Association of Secondary School Principals.

Valentine, J. W., & Mogar, D. C., (1992). Middle level certification: An encouraging evolution, *Middle School Journal, 24*(2),36-43.

Yerian, S. Y. & Grossman, P. L. (1993, April). Emerging themes on the effectiveness of teacher preparation through professional development schools. Paper presented at the American Educational Research Association, Atlanta.

Zeichner, K. M. (1992). Educating teachers for cultural diversity. Madison, WI: Wisconsin Center for Education Research, Unpublished paper.

Middle School Teacher Survey

❖ 1993 ❖

The Center for Early Adolescence, in cooperation with National Middle School Association, and with funding from the DeWitt Wallace-Reader's Digest Fund, is conducting this survey as a follow-up to its 1991 study of middle grades teacher preparation. The purpose of the study is to find out more about the preparation of teachers in states which have significant numbers of undergraduate and graduate middle level teacher preparation programs.

Your school has been selected to participate in this five-state survey. We are asking language arts, science, mathematics, and social studies teachers in grades 6, 7, and 8 to describe the kind of preparation they received for teaching in middle schools.

The survey will take only a few minutes to complete. We realize that your time is valuable and limited, and want you to know that your responses will help to strengthen the preparation of the nation's middle school teachers.

We have asked your principal to distribute the surveys to the appropriate teachers in your school. Along with the survey, you should have received a self-addressed, postage-paid envelope in which to mail the survey directly back to us.

Thank you very much for your contribution to this study. Your cooperation is very much appreciated.

Peter C. Scales, Ph.D.
Research Associate Professor
Center for Early Adolescence
University of North Carolina at Chapel Hill

C. Kenneth McEwin, Ed.D.
Professor
Appalachian State University
Boone, North Carolina

Middle School Teacher Survey

1993

NOTE: Middle grades is defined as grades 5 through 9.

Please circle your choices.

Section One—Demographic Information

1. Gender:
   a. Female   b. Male

2. Ethnicity:
   a. African American/Black
   b. Asian/Pacific Islander
   c. Latino/Hispanic
   d. Native American/Alaska Native
   e. White
   f. Other

3. Area in which school is located:
   a. Urban
   b. Suburban
   c. Rural

4. How long have you been a middle grades teacher?
   a. 1-3 years
   b. 4-9 years
   c. 10-14 years
   d. 15 years or more

5. What subject(s) do you regularly teach? (Circle all that apply.)
   a. English/Language Arts
   b. Mathematics
   c. Science
   d. Social Studies
   e. Reading
   f. Other

   Please specify "other" subjects taught: ____________________

6. Have you ever served as an elementary (K-4) or senior high school (10-12) teacher?
   a. Yes, elementary
   b. Yes, secondary
   c. Yes, both levels
   d. No

7. If you have been an elementary and/or secondary teacher, how many years did you teach at each level?

   Elementary
   a. 1-3 years
   b. 4-9 years
   c. 10-14 years
   d. 15 years or more

   Secondary
   a. 1-3 years
   b. 4-9 years
   c. 10-14 years
   d. 15 years or more

8. Was the professional preparation that resulted in your *initial* teacher certification elementary, middle level, or secondary (for example, mathematics or vocational education), or some other program?
   a. Elementary
   b. Middle Level
   c. Secondary
   d. Other, please specify ____________

9. *If different* from your initial preparation, was your most recent professional preparation elementary, middle level, secondary, or some other program?
   a. Elementary c. Secondary
   b. Middle Level d. Other, please specify ____________

10. When you selected teaching as a career goal, did you intend to become a middle grades teacher?
    a. Yes b. No

11. Did you receive your undergraduate preparation in a program specifically designed for middle grades teaching?
    a. Yes b. No

12. If you did not receive your professional preparation in a program specifically designed for prospective middle grades teachers, was a specialized middle level teacher preparation program available at the time?
    a. Yes b. No c. Do not know

13. At what institution(s) did you receive your professional preparation and what degrees did you receive?

Name of Institution	Degree Received
____________	____________
____________	____________
____________	____________
____________	____________
____________	____________

14. Please indicate the years you received your degree(s).
    a. Bachelors ________ c. Specialist ________
    b. Masters ________ d. Doctoral ________

15. Please indicate the type(s) of middle level teaching certificate (license) you hold including grade levels and subject areas as appropriate (for example, 6-8 mathematics):
    Grade Level(s) ________ Subject(s) ________
    Grade Level(s) ________ Subject(s) ________
    Grade Level(s) ________ Subject(s) ________

16. Please indicate below the number of courses and the total number of quarter or semester hours of your professional preparation that *focused directly on teaching in the middle grades* (grades 5-9).

    [Note: Please use the *first degree* you received that resulted in being certified to teach in the middle grades and *do not include student teaching hours* in the total. Please estimate if you do not remember exact numbers.]

    Number of specialized middle level courses: ____________

    Semester hours ____________ OR Quarter hours ____________

17. Please indicate which, if any, of the following was included in your professional preparation. (Please circle as many as apply.):

    a. Course work focusing directly on the developmental characteristics and needs of young adolescents (ages 10-15).

    b. Course work focusing directly on the curriculum and organization of the middle level school.

    c. Course work focusing directly on appropriate methods for teaching young adolescents.

    d. Course work focusing on teaching reading at the middle level.

    e. A broad academic background including concentrations in at least two academic areas at the undergraduate level and/or one at the graduate level.

    f. Pre-student teaching field experiences in the middle grades (grades 5-9).

       Please specify which grade or grades ______________

    g. Student teaching in the middle grades (grades 5-9).

       Please specify which grade or grades ______________

18. Do you intend to continue to teach at the middle level for the remainder of your career as an educator?

    a. Yes   b. No

    Why or why not? ____

    ____

Section Two—Professional Preparation

19. How well did your professional education programs prepare you for each of the following?

	Very Well	Adequately	Inadequately	Poorly	Not at all
a. Understanding young adolescent development (10-15 year olds).					
b. Using effective instructional techniques at the middle level.					
c. Middle level curriculum and organization.					
d. Teaching on an interdisciplinary team.					
e. Being an advisor in a teacher-based guidance program.					
f. Responding to students' cultural and language diversity.					
g. Using effective cooperative learning/grouping practices.					

20. Did your academic/content course work provide you with a satisfactory knowledge base for your subject specialty?
    a. Yes   b. No

21. Please indicate which, if any, of the following academic concentrations were included in your initial preparation.
    a. English/Language Arts   c. Mathematics
    b. Social Studies   d. Science

22. Were your academic/content concentrations broad and interdisciplinary in nature? (For example, science not biology; social studies not history.)
    a. Yes   b. No

Section Three—Your Perspectives

23. Are there important ideas, principles, or understandings that an effective middle level teacher needs to know?
    a. Yes   b. No

24. If yes, please list three examples of these ideas, principles, or understandings:

    ____

    ____

    ____

25. Please list three differences in the ways that middle level teachers should be prepared to teach compared with the ways that elementary/secondary teachers ought to be prepared.

    ____

    ____

    ____

26. Please list three changes that you feel could improve the preparation of middle level teachers.

    ____

    ____

    ____

27. Are you an individual member or is your school an institutional member of National Middle School Association?
    a. Yes, individual member
    b. Yes, member through school institutional membership
    c. No

    Why or why not? ____

____
____
____
____

28. Comments:

____
____
____
____
____
____
____
____
____
____
____
____
____
____
____
____

Thank you for your contribution to this study. Please return the survey in the self-addressed postage paid envelope.

Center for Early Adolescence
UNC-Chapel Hill
D-2 Carr Mill Town Center
Carrboro, NC 27510

Center for Early Adolescence

University of North Carolina at Chapel Hill
D-2 Carr Mill Town Center • Carrboro, North Carolina 27510 • (919) 966-1148
FAX • (919) 966-7657

Dear Middle School Principal:

The Center for Early Adolescence, in cooperation with National Middle School Association, and with funding from the DeWitt Wallace-Reader's Digest Fund, is conducting a new survey as a follow-up to its 1991 study of middle grades teacher preparation. The purpose of the study is to find out more about the professional preparation of middle school teachers in states which have significant numbers of specialized middle level undergraduate and graduate programs.

Your school has been selected to participate in this five-state study of middle school teachers. We realize that your time and that of teachers at your school is limited and valuable, and want you to know that your school's participation will help strengthen the preparation of the nation's middle school teachers.

We have enclosed six (6) brief surveys to be completed by six teachers at your school. Please select these six teachers from those who teach language arts, science, mathematics, and social studies in grades 6, 7, and 8. We suggest that you select teachers that reflect a variety of subject areas and grade levels. It should take them only a few minutes to complete these surveys. Six self-addressed, postage-paid envelopes are enclosed in which teachers should return their completed surveys.

Please return the enclosed post card to us after indicating how many teachers received surveys in which grade levels and in which subject areas. This information is very important to us since it is our only means of knowing how many teachers actually received a survey. If a teacher teaches more than one subject area, please count him or her as teaching the subject he or she teaches most frequently. When a teacher teaches more than one subject and teaches each equal amounts of time, count him or her in one subject area chosen at random rather than counting him or her twice. The same procedure should be followed if a teacher teaches more than one grade level.

Thank you very much for your important contribution. If you have questions, please do not hesitate to call us.

Peter C. Scales, Ph.D.
Research Associate Professor
Center for Early Adolescence
University of North Carolina at Chapel Hill

C. Kenneth McEwin, Ed.D.
Professor
Appalachian State University
Boone, North Carolina

Appendix B

Center for Early Adolescence

University of North Carolina at Chapel Hill
D-2 Carr Mill Town Center • Carrboro, North Carolina 27510 • (919) 966-1148
FAX • (919) 966-7657

Dear Principal:

Last month, we sent you a survey of middle school teachers' view on their preservice preparation developed by the Center for Early Adolescence with the cooperation of National Middle School Association. We have been gratified by the response to date: more than 1,200 teachers have returned completed questionnaires.

We are concerned, however, that we have not received any questionnaires from teachers at your school, nor have we received the postcard principals were to complete showing us which teachers (by content and grade level) you gave the questionnaires to. This information is very important for us to assess the adequacy of our response rate.

We know how hectic this time of year can be. However, this research will help shape middle-grades teacher preparation policy, and we sincerely hope that your teachers' voices can add to the importance of the study.

We encourage you to take a few minutes to select up to six teachers and give them the questionnaire, and check off which teachers you have chosen on the postcard we sent.

We know that you might already have given the questionnaires out. If so, we would appreciate your sending us the postcard indicating which teachers received the surveys, and reminding your teachers to complete the questionnaire. If the postcard or the questionnaires have been misplaced, please call us and we will be glad to send you additional copies.

Thank you so much for your interest and your support. We look forward to hearing from you.

Sincerely,

Peter C. Scales. Ph.D.
Research Associate Professor
University of North Carolina
at Chapel Hill

C. Kenneth McEwin, Ed.D.
Professor
Appalachian State
University

Advisory Panel
(Affiliation as of the start of the project March 1992)

Theodore E. Andrews
Professional Education and Certification
Washington State Department of Education

Ronald Areglado
Associate Executive Director of Programs
National Association of Elementary School Principals

Joan Baratz-Snowden
Vice President of Assessment and Research
National Board for Professional Teaching Standards

Ron Barber
Executive Director for Middle School Administration
Jefferson County, KY, Public Schools

William Bloomfield
Director, Center for Corporate and Education Initiatives
Brandeis University

Stephanie Burnkrant
President
National Collegiate Middle School Association (NCMSA)

Robby Champion
President
Champion Training and Consulting
Ellicott City, MD

Robert Chase
Vice President
National Education Association

Michael J. Cleary
Coordinator, Health Education Program
Department of Allied Health
Slippery Rock University

Donna V. Dunlop
Program Director
DeWitt Wallace-Reader's Digest Fund

Carolyn V. Eades
Head, Department of Mathematics
West Baltimore Middle School

Joyce Epstein
Center on Families, Communities,
Schools and Children's Learning
The Johns Hopkins University

Thomas 0. Erb
Associate Professor, Department of
Curriculum and Instruction
University of Kansas

Mary Ellen Finch
Division Chair, Education
Maryville University, St. Louis

Joni E. Finney
Director of Policy Studies
Education Commission of the States

Joseph J. Galbo
Professor of Education
California State University-Stanislaus

Maria Garza-Lubeck
MGSSPI Project Manager
Council of Chief State School Officers

Caroline Gaston
Education Policy Advisor
Office of the Governor, New Mexico

Nathalie Gehrke
Associate Professor, Education
University of Washington

Lynn Godwin
Teacher's College
Columbia University

Donna M. Gollnick
Deputy Executive Director
National Council for the Accreditation
of Teacher Education

Lillian Gonzalez
Deputy Superintendent
Baltimore City Public Schools

Anita H. Hall
Professor of Elementary Education
Jackson State University

David Haselkorn
President
Recruiting New Teachers, Inc.

Robert D. Hilliard
Associate Professor
University of Central Arkansas

David G. Imig
Chief Executive Officer
American Association of Colleges for
Teacher Education

Bruce Anthony Jones
Institute for Practice and
Research in Education
University of Pittsburgh

Gail Jones
School of Education
University of North Carolina at
Chapel Hill

Toni Griego Jones
Professor, Department of Curriculum
and Instruction
University of Wisconsin - Milwaukee

Laurel Martin Kanthak
Director of Middle Level Education
National Association of Secondary
School Principals

Eugenia Kemble
Assistant to the President
American Federation of Teachers

John H. Lounsbury
Publications Editor
National Middle School Association

M. Lee Manning
Darden College of Education
Old Dominion University

Robert M. McClure
Director, Mastery in
Learning Consortium
National Education Association

G. Williamson McDiarmid
National Center for Research on
Teacher Learning
Michigan State University

C. Kenneth McEwin, Jr.,
Professor of Education
Appalachian State University, NC

D. John McIntyre
Professor, Curriculum and Instruction
Southern Illinois University
at Carbondale

Edward J. Meade, Jr.
Independent Consultant
Montclair, NJ

Nicholas M. Michelli
Dean, School of Professional Studies
Montclair State College, NJ

Shirley L. Mow
Executive Director
Westchester Education Coalition, Inc.
White Plains, NY

Bertha 0. Pendleton
Deputy Superintendent
San Diego Unified School District

James Raths
Chair, Department of
Educational Studies
University of Delaware

Madeleine Ray
Director, Professional Development in Early Adolescence Program
Bank Street College, New York

Gloria Richeson
Assistant Superintendent for Middle Schools
Wake County, NC, Public Schools

Susan Riemer Sacks
Chair, Education Program
Barnard College
Columbia University

Joan Schine
Director, National Center for Service Learning in Early Adolescence, NYC

Carol A. Skinner
Teacher
Iroquois Middle School
Louisville, KY

Jackie M. Stanley
Coordinator, Minority Recruitment Programs
South Carolina Center for Teacher Recruitment

Donald J. Stedman
Dean, School of Education
University of North Carolina at Chapel Hill

John H. Swaim
Professor of Education
University of Northern Colorado

Belle R. Tomasello
Cooperative Learning Implementer
Parkman Middle School
Milwaukee Public Schools

Samuel Totten
Center for Middle Level Education, Research, and Development
University of Arkansas

Efrain Vila
Principal
Kosciuszko Middle School
Milwaukee, WI

At-Large Members

Joan Lipsitz
Program Director, Education
Lilly Endowment, Inc.

M. Hayes Mizell
Director, Program for Disadvantaged Youth
The Edna McConnell Clark Foundation

Anthony W. Jackson
Program Officer
Carnegie Corporation of New York